The South Lives in History

Southern Historians and Their Legacy

By WENDELL HOLMES STEPHENSON

GREENWOOD PRESS, PUBLISHERS
NEW YORK

To Lamar Voyles Stephenson

A SON OF THE SOUTH

Contents

Preface

AN INVITATION to deliver the Walter Lynwood Fleming Lectures in Southern History at Louisiana State University gave the speaker opportunity to return to a campus where eighteen happy and busy years were devoted to the promotion of southern history, and to a region in which he lived for nearly thirty years. A native of the Middle West, his cordial reception below Mason and Dixon's line, first in a border state and then in the deep South, inspired a desire to understand Southerners—white and Negro—and their ways of life and work. The task was not difficult, for the southern world is quite different when viewed from the inside than when observed at long range from across the frontier. Too often Southerners are appraised solely in relationship to issues currently in public attention, whether in the 1850's or the 1950's.

History is too much a record of clash and conflict, too little a matter of harmonious living, of affairs great and small that affect daily lives more tangibly than political and constitutional issues. Sometimes history provides a battlefield or a forum, where sword meets sword or mind meets mind, for men have ever differed on rights and policies. But a clash and conflict emphasis in the writing of history, whether of the South or any other part of the world, produces a distorted picture. Studies of the 1850's, recent and remote, concentrate upon clashes of rival partisans, the question of slavery and the problem of race, competition of agriculture and industry, the struggle between moderatism and fanaticism. These are important segments of history, but the reader may conclude that Americans of a century ago gave little attention to other aspects of human endeavor. As a matter of fact, they led normal, wholesome lives as they went about their daily tasks of plowing and planting and harvesting, of manufacturing and mining and transporting, of teaching and preaching and playing, of the hundred and one items that combine into a mosaic of individual personality or collective society. Southerners have been personified in terms of conflict: nullification, sectionalism, slavery, secession, civil war, hooded orders, and the race problem. Many have worn such clothing, but it is not workaday apparel. Controversial issues are sometimes at attention's focus, more often on its periphery.

This is a book about the writing of southern history and some of the men who wrote it. Like the men who made history, those who recorded it sometimes engaged in clash and conflict, but for the most part they endeavored to set down faithfully what the sources yielded. History written in the generation following Appomattox, they believed, dealt unjustly with the South, and they would therefore revise it. Strive as they might for impartiality, they could not attain it, for they labored in an atmosphere still charged with a remnant of sectionalism; and a later generation has been re-evaluating old evidence and discovering new sources that permit a reappraisal.

Historiography is, however, cumulative as well as innovative: cumulative in that many of the findings of earlier generations are carried forward in revisions; innovative because some of the accumulation is rejected as inaccurate or prejudiced, new questions are directed to the records, and unused data become available. But the cumulative quality makes it worthwhile to study the teachings and writings of the last generation's historians, for much of the

knowledge and some of the interpretations are as valid today as they were twenty-five or fifty years ago. The sensational cult would ignore the heritage, or pretend to. Some
of the innovations that correct or modify or expand the
work of the pioneers are suggested in the pages that follow;
a detailed consideration of them would require a volume
much longer than this one.

Believing in the cumulative value of historiography,
the writer began a study of southern historians several years
ago. Essays on three of them—William E. Dodd, Ulrich B.
Phillips, and Walter Lynwood Fleming—are printed substantially as they were delivered as lectures. The intro-
ductory chapter was written subsequently to place the three
in the context of the period in which they taught and wrote.
Certain criteria were employed in presenting them and
their contributions: they should be permitted to speak for
themselves, through their writings and letters; they should
be evaluated as their contemporaries measured them; and
they should be critically appraised as of today. Phillips
and Fleming delved deeper into the sources than Dodd,
but he succeeded better than they in freeing himself of
southernism.

The essays on Dodd and Phillips each comprised over a
hundred pages in early drafts; compressing to lecture
length excluded some significant aspects of their careers.
In still briefer form the chapter on Dodd was read at a dinner meeting of the Mississippi Valley Historical Association. Subsequently it was accepted for publication in the
Virginia Quarterly Review, but the editor kindly permitted
withdrawal so that it could be re-expanded into one of the
lectures. Some years ago the writer published a brief paper
on Fleming in the *Alabama Review,* October, 1948; his
thanks are due to the editor for permission to draw upon it,
and also upon articles on George Petrie, July, 1948, and

Thomas M. Owen, January, 1949, in the preparation of the present essay.

Much of the material for all of the chapters was assembled in 1944–45 while the writer held a research grant from the General Education Board, to whom he gratefully acknowledges obligation. In an effort to understand the historians treated herein, and their contemporaries about whom he has written already, he supplemented a study of their published works by an examination of their private papers. These, he hopes, have contributed to a personalized account which printed pages could not provide. The manuscript collections of historians, living and deceased, were opened to him without restriction. Collections of personal papers are listed in the bibliography, but two of them should be mentioned here because of special courtesies in their use. To Mrs. Alfred K. (Martha Dodd) Stern the writer is grateful not only for access to her father's papers, then housed in the Stern country home near Ridgefield, Connecticut, but also for a hermit's lodgment while using them; and to the late Mrs. John Spencer Bassett for gracious entertainment in her Northampton, Massachusetts, home while examining her husband's collection. Many pages would be required for a complete recital of all the hospitalities the researcher received in Austin, Jackson, Montgomery, Tuscaloosa, Auburn, Atlanta, Decatur, Nashville, Columbia, Chapel Hill, Durham, Raleigh, Charlottesville, Richmond, Williamsburg, Falls Church, Arlington, Washington, Baltimore, New York, and Cambridge. Research can be pleasant, indeed. From former students and other acquaintances of the pioneers he received suggestions helpful in evaluating their historical stature. The writer also expresses thanks to the University of Oregon Research Council for a summer grant in 1954.

Some obligations for specific aid are acknowledged at appropriate places in the bibliography. For sundry tangible favors the writer is also indebted to Miss Susan B. Keane, reference secretary, and Mrs. Florence W. Toppino, registrar, Tulane University; James Walter Mason, Atlanta, Georgia; Roland M. Harper, University, Alabama; E. Merton Coulter and Robert P. Brooks, University of Georgia; and Fulmer Mood, University of Texas. My competent research assistant, Miss Virginia E. Orkney, has given time and talent generously to completion of the essays and compilation of the bibliography.

W. H. S.

Eugene, Oregon
June 15, 1955

THE SOUTH LIVES IN HISTORY

CHAPTER ONE

The Southern Avenue to Now

As THE NINETEENTH CENTURY faded into the twentieth a long lifetime ago, pioneer historians of the South were laying foundations upon which later scholars built a history of the land called Dixie. The work of the pioneers was largely accomplished in the first quarter of the new century, and the decade of the late twenties and early thirties served as a watershed between the years of origins and an age of maturity. The thousands of volumes of southern history and biography on library shelves in 1955, and the far greater number of articles in professional journals and popular magazines, are tangible evidence that the South lives in history.

I

Scholarly treatment of the South's past antedated the turn of the century by a decade or two. The initial institutional impulse developed at Johns Hopkins University, whither Herbert Baxter Adams attracted graduates of southern colleges and universities. Despite deficiencies as teacher and researcher, Adams was, as Woodrow Wilson described him, "a great Captain of Industry, a captain in the field of systematic and organized scholarship." The interests of this German-educated New Englander were not primarily in the region below Mason and Dixon's line, but his sympathetic attitude toward Southerners and their research problems, a growing collection of historical materials relating to the South, the location of the university in Baltimore, and special fellowships available to residents of Maryland, Virginia, and North Carolina created an impression that the Department of Historical and Political Science was peculiarly southern. Appropriately enough, the first systematic course in the history of the South was inaugurated at Hopkins.

More than a score of southern scholars received their doctorates under Adams' direction and performed creditably in the South following graduation. Some of them became forgotten men as their services receded into the past; the names of others still live as dynamic contributors to an incipient southern historiography. John Spencer Bassett at Trinity College, George Petrie at Alabama Polytechnic Institute, St. George L. Sioussat at the University of the South and at Vanderbilt, and Franklin L. Riley at the University of Mississippi were Hopkins-trained men to whom Adams imparted a zealous enthusiasm for academic improvement in the South. Woodrow Wilson's work was chiefly on northern soil and primarily in political science, but his reinterpretation of American history was an important landmark in a better balanced treatment of the nation's past. William P. Trent, who left Hopkins before attaining the doctorate, found southern history at Sewanee an inviting field before abandoning it in 1900 for a professorship in English literature at Columbia University.

Perhaps no southern scholars trained in history at Hopkins attained the stature of Frederick Jackson Turner, J. Franklin Jameson, or Charles M. Andrews, but several of them inaugurated activities in the South that eventually advanced genuine historical scholarship. They taught courses in local and regional history, assembled the raw materials of their craft in libraries and archives, wrote prolifically on southern subjects, and established media for the publication of their studies and those of their students. In all of these activities they were emulating the example set by their Hopkins mentor. Like their northern and western contemporaries, they found a welcome avenue to the printed page in the Hopkins *Studies in Historical and Political Science* to supplement a variety of other outlets for their writings. By the beginning of the new century fifty-three Southerners trained at Hopkins had published more than three hundred books, monographs, and other shorter pieces on the South, and men from other sections had contributed over fifty articles on southern subjects to periodicals.

While conservatism dominated the thinking of many southern historians in the pioneer period, it was a conservatism that contrasted at least mildly with prevailing thought in the South. Two Hopkins men, Trent and Bassett, were decidedly liberal in their views. Dissatisfied with the intellectual backwardness of their region, each founded a quarterly magazine to provide a forum for literary criticism and liberal thought. The *Sewanee Review*, established at the University of the South in 1892, and the *South Atlantic Quarterly*, inaugurated at Trinity College a decade later, were permanent legacies of Trent and Bassett. Meritorious magazines at their inception, they are still highly esteemed after an unbroken existence of two generations.

Trent's study of English culture in the Old Dominion, his biographies of William Gilmore Simms and Robert E. Lee, his pen portraits of Old South statesmen, and sundry articles in professional and popular periodicals brought him recognition as a historian before he transferred to Columbia University. With the exception of the Simms biography, these works did not long survive, but Trent's critical quarterly and his liberal preachments were important milestones in the development of southern thought and culture. Neither regional nor partisan, the *Sewanee Review* sought to achieve those ends through a broad interpretation of its function. Walter H. Page's project to report sectional civilizations in the *Atlantic Monthly* suggested Trent as the appropriate portrayer of the South fully as much as Turner for an analysis of the West. The Sewanee scholar's articles on "Dominant Forces in Southern Life" and "Tendencies of Higher Life in the South" stressed the region's cultural pattern in the 1890's against a perspective of the Old South regime. An advocate of self-criticism as the basis of an enduring literature, he saw great potentiality in southern colleges whose faculties included a growing number of young liberals educated in German and northern universities. The critical spirit, he thought, had permeated history more than any other field. But he grew weary of pioneering from his mountain fastness in eastern Tennessee. Progress toward enlightenment was too slow. "Shallow thinking on political matters, provincialism of taste & sentiments—ignorance & vanity are the dominant characteristics of our people," he wrote in assigning motives for desiring to leave the South.

Bassett, too, left the South after a dozen years at Trinity College, and for similar reasons. His publications on North Carolina and Virginia history, useful in the training of a historian but otherwise relatively insignificant, were overshadowed by his liberal teachings and the launching of a forum in which he and his contemporaries could express themselves unreservedly. He inspired in his students a Jeffersonian desire "to follow truth wherever it may lead," even though it undermined southern tradition. "Let us conduct ourselves," Bassett urged, "that the world may know that there is in the South at least one spot in which our history may be presented in all of its claims, and where it may receive a respectful and unimpassioned hearing." In the spirit of "liberty to think" he established the *South Atlantic Quarterly* in 1902 to promote "literary, historical, and social development." His own editorials stressed the literary backwardness and political intolerance of the

South, and he suggested remedies for "poverty of scholarship" and shallow culture. History as well as criticism found an important place in the quarterly. Bassett himself contributed historical articles, and such young historians as Dodd, Phillips, and Fleming found it a convenient medium for their wares.

In leaving the South for northern institutions, Bassett and Trent were exceptions to the rule, for most of the southern historians trained at Hopkins remained in the South to contribute in a less spectacular way to the gradual evolution of historical scholarship. With Adams' death in 1901, the Baltimore university lost priority as a mecca for Southerners, although acquisition of the doctorate by Douglas Southall Freeman and Hamilton J. Eckenrode after the turn of the century indicates that prestige did not cease abruptly. William A. Dunning declined the position as Adams' successor and thereby assured primacy to Columbia University in the historical training of southern scholars in the first two decades of the twentieth century.

The leadership which Dunning afforded stemmed from competent teaching and authoritative articles assembled for publication in 1898 as *Essays on the Civil War and Reconstruction.* His *Reconstruction, Political and Economic,* published a few years later, enhanced a well-established reputation for sympathetic treatment of the South in a controversial era. Services to graduate students in history were not limited to those who specialized in this epoch, but his name became synonymous with the direction of dissertations on the Civil War and Reconstruction. An able group of southern students joined his "school." He "was indeed aware," he informed contributors to *Studies in Southern History and Politics,* "that fate was favoring Columbia and its Department of History with a most earnest, inspiring and generally attractive body of students, to assist whom was pedagogic joy."

Among this able array of Southerners who wrote their dissertations on the Civil War–Reconstruction epoch were James W. Garner, Walter L. Fleming, J. G. de Roulhac Hamilton, Charles W. Ramsdell, C. Mildred Thompson, William Watson Davis, and Thomas S. Staples. Like their master, they revised the nineteenth-century view of Reconstruction, for in general they sympathized with the white South and thereby inspired later scholars to revise their revisions. But their contributions to scholarship, and those of Ulrich B. Phillips, Milledge L. Bonham, and Paul Leland Haworth, were valuable achievements in the early years of the twentieth century. Some of their dissertations did not approach objectivity as closely as theses written in the eighties and nineties under Adams' direction, but their investigations were broader and deeper. Research and writing advanced considerably in the transition from the Baltimore to the New York center of southern activity. In one respect, at least, precedent was followed: many of the Southerners trained in Dunning's seminar returned to the South to teach state and regional history, to assemble historical materials in libraries and archives, to continue research and writing, and to inspire another generation of students with a desire to investigate the South's past. Phillips in particular passed the torch of historical scholarship to a large number of students; Hamilton provided an enduring monument in assembling a great manuscript collection; and Fleming outdistanced his master in investigating the Reconstruction era.

II

Looking backward is a human characteristic that manifests itself in group activity as well as in individual endeavor. State and local historical societies in the South, as in other regions, antedated the Civil War, and the domestic conflict of the sixties gave Southerners special events to record and justify. The preservation of the South's role in the War for Southern Independence led to the founding of the Southern Historical Society at New Orleans in 1869, with Confederate generals prominent in personnel and in official positions. After a few years in the Crescent City, the society was reorganized with headquarters in Richmond; and in 1876 it began the publication of the Southern Historical Society *Papers*. Its purpose was the assembling and preservation of Confederate records, the source materials that some future historian would use in writing a history of the Confederacy. Some important documents were printed in the *Papers*, along with reminiscences and apologias of participants, to win the battle of history as partial compensation for the Lost Cause. The enthusiastic leadership that Douglas Southall Freeman gave the society enhanced its contribution to Confederate history.

The society's concentration on the Civil War period prompted a younger group of men, some of them trained in graduate schools, to form the Southern History Association in 1896. Veterans gave the new organization some support, diplomats and government employees contributed desultory interest, and college professors and administrators provided a scholarly nucleus. With headquarters in Washington, members of the new society inaugurated *Publications*, which appeared regularly for a decade. The editor, Colyer Meriwether, supplemented fees with his own resources to give the association financial stability, but a membership list of a little over two hundred discouraged a continuation of private support. A plan to merge the organization with the American Historical Association and continue the *Publications* failed to materialize, and the Southern History Association issued its last number in 1907. Scholarly articles on all periods of southern history were published in its volumes, some significant documents were included, and books were critically appraised. Editor Meriwether, a Hopkins doctor of philosophy, belittled the prevailing concept of research and writing in graduate schools. His diatribes against the dry-as-dust dissertations emanating from Hopkins and other universities were early expressions of a justifiable criticism. The formless monographic content of "scientific" history served no useful purpose, he thought, for the great synthesizers of the day ignored these examples of futility.

Meanwhile, historians of the South were finding the American Historical Association a congenial atmosphere. A landmark in that direction was a session on southern history at the Washington meeting in 1901. Lyon G. Tyler of William and Mary College read a paper on the history of the London Company records, John S. Bassett of Trinity College discussed the relations between the Virginia planter and the London merchants, William E. Dodd of Randolph-Macon College presented Nathaniel Macon's place in southern history, Bernard C. Steiner of Johns Hopkins analyzed Maryland's early courts, and George P. Garrison of the University of Texas stressed his own university's activities in describing the work of studying and writing history under way in the Southwest. At the close of the session members interested in the history of the South discussed the teaching of the subject in their region and the feasibility of forming a southern section of the association. The conference decided against a formal organization but agreed to examine the teaching of history in the South.

The chairmanship of a committee to investigate the status of historical instruction was assigned to Frederick W. Moore of Vanderbilt University. Correspondence with other members of the committee, a study of college catalogues, and a questionnaire directed to each of the schools revealed that there were over sixty degree-granting institutions in southern states, that each of them provided at least one course in history, and that sixteen offered more than twelve hours in the subject. It was discouraging to learn, however, that in more than fifty institutions the teacher of history also instructed in other subjects, and that some of the history classes were inadequately taught. The recent inauguration of courses by young men with degrees from recognized American and European universities and the large number of Southerners working for the doctorate at reputable schools were hopeful signs.

An incipient feeling of unity among historians of the South was accompanied by an ambition to attract the association to a southern city for an annual meeting. Vanderbilt University, with the endorsement of several southern members and many from the North, offered to serve as host in 1902. Dunning presented Nashville's invitation, but the council hesitated to migrate so far from the geographical center of membership, even though the object was a promotion of historical activity in the South. The council was open-minded on the subject, however, and continued pressure from northern as well as southern members brought a decision to meet at New Orleans in 1903, the centennial of the Louisiana Purchase.

Scholarly historians of the South were elated at this opportunity to welcome the national organization to a southern city, but several factors prevented a large attendance from the region. As Moore's report demonstrated, the number of full-time teachers of history in southern colleges and universities was still small, heavy teaching loads and low salaries were prevailing attributes that circumscribed the mental horizons of several teachers, and travel funds were almost nonexistent. Consequently, the number of historians from all the southern states did not exceed the total from Massachusetts. But the enthusiasm of Southerners who did attend was a compensating factor, and the ultimate effect of the meeting may have been greater than contemporaries supposed. And, if correspondence may serve as an index, historians from other sections were thrilled with the prospect of assembling in the most cosmopolitan city in the United States and gratified with their cordial reception in the deep South. A special train brought Northeasterners from New York City to New Orleans, with stopovers at Richmond, Atlanta, and Montgomery. For some unexplainable reason no effort was made to welcome delegates in Richmond and Atlanta, and the hours they tarried in those cities were dull indeed; but the reception in Montgomery was a pleasant memory that lingered long in their minds.

The historian who sparked the Montgomery reception was Thomas M. Owen, already recognized throughout the country for pioneer work in archival organization and administration. First as secretary of the Alabama Historical Society and then as director of the State Department of Archives and History, he provided dynamic and energetic leadership, the department soon became a model followed by other states, and Owen received national acclaim. Historians and economists, who met concurrently in New Orleans, were delighted with his arrangements for acquainting them with the Confederacy's first capitol. "The memory of the Southern trip is a joy to all of us," George L. Beer wrote after returning home, "and we shall not soon . . . forget that moonlight night in Montgomery and the guide who made the noble old city's past so charmingly alive for us." Dunning reported to Fleming, who had not attended the meeting, that "your enterprising friend, Owen, at Montgomery, made a particularly good impression for himself; he treated us royally well. When the train stopped there at 9:30 in the evening, the old state house was impressively and entertainingly exhibited by him, and his whole spirit, both there and at New Orleans, won him a host of friends in the Association and at the same time, I think won for the Association a very earnest friend in him." Writing to Owen, James Ford Rhodes reported that "the History and Economic people have not yet got over talking of your speech in the moonlight on the Capitol."

Two of the New Orleans sessions had a southern theme. One of them consisted of papers relating to the Louisiana Purchase; the other, arranged by Dunning, considered "The Study and Teaching of History in the South." Two northern historians, Jameson of the University of Chicago and Lucy M. Salmon of Vassar College, participated in the discussion; and seven Southerners, Dodd, Moore, Owen, Riley, David Y. Thomas of Arkansas, Alcée Fortier of Tulane, and Lilian W. Johnson of Tennessee, made brief reports. Despite a paucity of members from the South, the conference was well attended—and decidedly successful, if contemporary correspondence may be believed. Dunning thought that Dodd had presented a too pessimistic picture of historical activity in the South; but in general the reports indicated that progress was under way.

In the years that followed, Southerners became more active in association meetings, although membership in the South continued to be relatively small. The society's council appointed Bassett a member of the general committee in 1902, and he retained this position for several years. Occasionally a southern member was elected to the council or appointed to some committee. Scholarly papers on southern subjects were accepted for publication in the *Review* if they met Jameson's exacting standards. Richmond shared with Washington the responsibility of host to the association in 1908. Another landmark in southern interest occurred in 1913 when the annual meeting was held in Charleston; Dunning's presidency that year brought many of his devotees to South Carolina's historic city. The association returned to the South three times in subsequent years: to Richmond in 1924, to Durham and Chapel Hill in 1929, and to Chattanooga in 1935. Rapid growth of the society with concentration of membership in the North-east and inadequate hotel facilities in southern cities pre-vented periodic meetings in the South. Soon after the founding of the Southern Historical Association in the 1930's, joint sessions with the American Historical Associa-tion stimulated southern interest in the national organiza-tion.

III

The association council's decision to hold the 1903 meeting in New Orleans may have inspired Edwin A. Alderman, president of Tulane University, to search for the distinguishing southern characteristics in American life. Somewhat unconsciously, southern writers had ap-proached this theme in the preceding generation, usually in a controversial atmosphere. A notable exception was Basil L. Gildersleeve, professor of Greek for twenty years at the University of Virginia before transferring to Hop-kins in 1876. With a Carolina background and Confederate experience, Gildersleeve received a formal education at Princeton and at German universities which attuned a scholarly mind to independent thought without destroying either faith in or respect for his native Southland. When in the 1890's he published "The Creed of the Old South" and "A Southerner in the Peloponnesian War" in the *Atlantic Monthly,* a southern gentleman was speaking not in defense but in explanation. A knowledge of political and military conflicts of antiquity enabled him to write in humanizing context and historical perspective. He said little about slavery as a cause of the conflict in which he participated, but he lingered over the obligation dilemma in the minds of Virginians and South Carolinians on the eve of secession.

Civil war could have been averted, a northern student had told him, if Southerners "had been of a statistical turn." There were enough Athenians and Southerners of that turn of mind, Gildersleeve thought, but temporal calculations of cost seemed unimpressive "when the things that are eternal"—submission to encroachment, incarnate principle and idea—forced themselves into consciousness a third of a century before. Volumes were published in the twentieth century on the Old South's creed and its sources, but no latter-day historian wrote with Gildersleeve's perspective and scholarly erudition. Present-day writers might well read the classical scholar's classic of the 1890's before they "discover" too many new approaches to the American conflict.

With noble intent but unsuccessful result Alderman sought to discover "the contributions made by southern stock and southern civilization to our American character." What made the South southern and its inhabitants Southerners? "What good things," distinctly southern, could "be relied upon to add strength and beauty to the national character?" These questions were propounded to thirty-five or more men and women, among them Hannis Taylor, Frederick Jackson Turner, David F. Houston, Ashton Phelps, Albert Shaw, Thomas Nelson Page, Grace King, Ellen Glasgow, Winston Churchill (a member of the New Hampshire legislature), and Henry Adams. As Alderman would use the biographical approach, he asked each correspondent to name a half-dozen Southerners who "typify the essential character contributions of the Southern States to the national life." A few of the names appeared in most of the responses—Washington, Jefferson, Madison, Marshall, Calhoun, Andrew Jackson, Lee, and Stonewall Jackson—but such names as Maury and Shreve, Poe and Lanier, and even Abraham Lincoln were nominated.

Apparently Alderman did not pursue his object further.

Some letters—particularly those of Turner and Adams—were discouraging. Turner claimed Jackson and Clay for the West; and while southern influences affected the careers of Washington, Jefferson, and Madison, their lives were merged in a national framework. Jefferson was western as well as southern. John Randolph and Calhoun and Lee and Yancey and Toombs and Stephens approximated the concept better than the more nationalized statesmen. Adams could give no assistance, for "southern society has left very little trace in literature of its own," and southern statesmen were self-conscious actors whose acting did not merit biographies. "Your business," he counseled, "is to be an artist—to make a picture,—to paint a character,—not to preach, or lecture, or flatter."

Houston, author of *Nullification in South Carolina* and president of Texas Agricultural and Mechanical College, unhesitatingly and romantically described the Southerner who contributed to national character. He was individualistic and conservative, gracious and courteous, dignified and self-respecting, incorruptible in private and public affairs, nonmercenary in his view of government, and broadminded in his attitude toward policies. Demonstrating "magnanimity in misfortune; moderation, patience, and fortitude in calamity," he had "a keen perception of honor, and a ready determination to take action, regardless of consequence, in behalf of great causes." Lee, Calhoun, and Stonewall Jackson embodied more of these traits than other Southerners. Admittedly the characteristics applied to the upper class in southern society; little was known of the other classes. Albert Shaw suggested "qualities of refinement, grace, loyalty" as particular attributes of southern women. Southern men had "an extraordinary talent for oratory," and they contributed a disproportionate share of "philosophical statesmanship." "I think," he added, "the South has also a better talent for imaginative literature than any other portion of the country." Hannis Taylor agreed in part. He was unimpressed with the South's legacy "in the field of serious literature"; its contributions lay in "the science of politics"—a "political and forensic" genius. "As constitution makers, as jurists, as diplomats, as tribunitian orators, the men of the South have been of the highest order."

Gildersleeve's creed and Alderman's correspondents were prophetic and suggestive. Conceptual and biographical approaches would be used by countless historians of the South during the next half century in serious endeavor to recapture the spirit of the past, the distinctiveness of southern life, and the role of the region in the national framework. Turner and Adams were thinking more sanely and pragmatically at the dawn of the new century; but they and their southern contemporaries could hardly comprehend what avenue to concepts and characteristics fifty years of delving would construct.

IV

The scholar who teaches and writes southern history in the 1950's has access to thousands of volumes treating all periods and many aspects of the region's history. A dozen or more state historical societies issue reputable quarterly magazines, and regional and national historical periodicals also print articles and collections of documents relating to the history of the South. The annual output of books and articles on southern history has become so large that specialists find it increasingly difficult to keep abreast of the field's literature.

In striking contrast, the pioneers of 1900 worked with limited resources. In the monographic area, the Columbia University *Studies in History, Economics and Public Law*, inaugurated in 1891, supplemented the Hopkins *Studies in*

Historical and Political Science, established eight years earlier. The Southern History Association *Publications* and a few short-lived annuals such as the Vanderbilt History Society *Publications* lodged shorter pieces, some of dubious value. Only a few of today's reputable historical magazines antedated the twentieth century. The *American Historical Review* and the *Political Science Quarterly* opened their issues to southern subjects; the *William and Mary College Quarterly* and the *Virginia Magazine of History and Biography* exhumed segments of the Old Dominion's past; the *American Historical Magazine and Tennessee Historical Society Quarterly* mingled trifle and treasure; and the *Quarterly of the Texas State Historical Association* focused attention on the South's western periphery.

In so brief a survey a sampling of the works on southern history available at the end of the nineteenth century must suffice. Philip A. Bruce published *The Plantation Negro as a Freeman* in 1889; the first of his trilogy on seventeenth-century Virginia—the *Economic History*—appeared in 1895. Alexander Brown's *Genesis of the United States* was published in 1890; the *First Republic in America* in 1898. *Old Virginia and Her Neighbours,* by John Fiske, reached the printed page in 1897. Despite superficiality it long remained a standard work. The first two segments of Edward McCrady's South Carolina trilogy—*South Carolina Under the Proprietary Government, 1670–1719,* and *South Carolina Under the Royal Government, 1719–1776* —were published in 1897 and 1899; the third, *South Carolina in the Revolution,* soon thereafter. David F. Houston's *Critical Study of Nullification in South Carolina* was issued in 1896. After a few minor studies, *Suppression of the African Slave-Trade to the United States of America* started W. E. B. Du Bois on a productive career the same year. Among Civil War works available by the end of the century were James D. Bulloch's *Secret Service of the Confederate States in Europe* (1884) and John T. Scharf's *History of the Confederate States Navy* (1887).

At least fifty biographies of Southerners were published during the last third of the century, but most of them were inadequate even by that period's standards. Among the better books were G. F. R. Henderson's *Stonewall Jackson and the American Civil War* (1898), Carl Schurz's *Henry Clay* (1887), and Lyon G. Tyler's *Letters and Times of the Tylers* (1884–96). The "Father of American Biography," James Parton, published *Andrew Jackson* in 1860 and *Thomas Jefferson* in 1874. William Wirt Henry's *Patrick Henry* appeared in 1891, John W. Du Bose's *Life and Times of William Lowndes Yancey* in 1892, William P. Trent's provocative but scholarly *William Gilmore Simms* in the same year, his *Southern Statesmen of the Old Régime* in 1897, and his *Robert E. Lee* in 1899. William Garrott Brown, literary historian and essayist of great promise, afflicted by deafness and tuberculosis, began his brilliant career in the 1890's by contributing articles to weekly and monthly periodicals and by publishing *Andrew Jackson* in 1900. Women writers joined the biographical parade with Kate Mason Rowland's *George Mason* in 1892 and Mrs. Harriott H. Ravenel's *Eliza Pinckney* in 1896.

The lists of biographies and other works could be greatly expanded but, even so, hiatus would dwarf catenation, quantity surpass quality. On first thought it might seem that the pioneers experienced little difficulty in reading all the books and articles on the South. Actually, heavy teaching loads that often included classes in European and English history, in one or more other social studies fields, or in literature and foreign languages precluded concentration.

And then came the era of Dodd and Phillips and Fleming and their contemporaries whose output swelled the volume of southern history far beyond the limits of 1900. Their academic children and grandchildren, with increasing respect for the canons of critical scholarship, made southern history an acceptable and usual part of American historiography. As an index of growth, the *American Historical Review* appraised a dozen volumes of southern history in 1900; the *Journal of Southern History* reviewed some fifty works in 1940.

The literature of controversy, to which many Southerners contributed in postwar years, was plentiful, but much of it was so unhistorical that its value to the scholar was dubious, except as it represented the history of opinion and sentiment. Some of the early twentieth-century historians labored in an atmosphere still charged with a remnant of sectional feeling, with conservative thought apparent in writings that emanated from the South. Southern historians were convinced that much history written in the North dealt unjustly with their region. A part of the unfairness was charged to distortion, another part to neglect. For dereliction Southerners assumed responsibility. A fair-minded historian who wrote in Boston or New York or Philadelphia did not have access to southern sources, and monographic studies were too few to provide much enlightenment. An obligation therefore rested upon Southerners to provide synthesizers and text writers with evidence that would encourage a better balanced and less partisan view of history.

The southern protest against distortion appeared occasionally in articles and books and reviews, more often in the private correspondence of scholars. Sectional feeling manifested itself in some of the letters, but a dominant note in many of them was a growing understanding of the southern problem and an appreciation among northern historians of a new scholarship developing in the South. Writing to Bassett after receiving a copy of the *South*

Atlantic Quarterly, Charles McLean Andrews of Bryn Mawr College asserted: "You have certainly undertaken a magnificent work in attempting to develop a more vital literary activity in the South and the result of your experiment will be watched with greatest interest and sympathy by every one who is concerned for the educational and literary future of this country. . . . I look with increasing admiration upon you men of the South, from North Carolina to Texas, for the enthusiasm and energy that you are all displaying in the endeavor, to show your historical colleagues of the Middle, North, and West that there is a great world south of Mason and Dixon's line, full of latent power and force, that needs only cultivation to show what it can accomplish."

That northern and southern thought on the war's aftermath was converging is well illustrated in correspondence between Charles Francis Adams and Henry G. Connor. These two men lifted their thinking above petty sectional animosity, and they frequently exchanged articles and addresses. Adams ingratiated himself with Virginia audiences on his visits to Lexington and Richmond. His address, "Lee's Centennial," brought widespread acclaim for the New Englander who numbered abolitionists among his ancestors. He could not concur in the northern "article of the established faith," he wrote to the North Carolinian in 1912, that the settlement following Appomattox was a soft peace. "Within a year I have heard it stated as something that did not admit of dispute that no 'conquered people' had ever experienced an equal degree of leniency at the hands of the victor. . . . On the contrary, I more and more think that rarely has any people been dealt with more severely." Despite "few imprisonments and no executions," punishment was nevertheless severe. To devastating and cruel experiences on the battlefield were added disfranchisement of the whites and the setting over them of "their newly enfranchised slaves of another and inferior race." Confiscation of slave property under a martial law proclamation represented the destruction of wealth which Adams estimated at $3,000,000,000. The government's pension system resulted in a long-time penalty for southern states, for they were forced through taxation to contribute toward the victors' pensions. The $800,000,000 paid by Southerners prior to 1912 was roughly the equivalent of the indemnity levied by victorious Germany on France following the Franco-Prussian War. "I fail to recall any case," Adams wrote, "where the vanquished party had a heavier fine inflicted upon it, and certainly there is no previous case in history where the recently enfranchised slave had conferred upon him full legislative power over his former master and owner." "Put it how you will," he added, "these are pretty severe articles of indictment!"

Such sentiments as these were indeed welcome to southern historians. Northern scholars were beginning to recognize an incipient scholarship in the South, and some of them were admitting that radical Reconstruction had been a mistake. But at this point another element entered the picture, for northern repudiation of postwar radical governments stirred Negro historians to militant defense of the role of their race in the tragic era. W. E. B. Du Bois and other Negro scholars were convinced that southern history was distorted and Negro contributions neglected. The problem of southern history was now tripartite rather than bisectional. The founding of the *Journal of Negro History* in 1916 gave historians and other social studies scholars a medium of expression that eventually contributed to a fuller appreciation of the constructive role played by a minority segment of southern society.

Northern recognition of southern scholarship was also evident in the migration of native historians of the South to colleges and universities in the Middle West and the Northeast. Trent, as we have seen, left the University of the South for Columbia University in 1900, at the same time abandoning a field which literature had already encroached upon; and Bassett accepted a position at Smith College in 1906. After eight years at Randolph-Macon College, Dodd was called to the University of Chicago; and Phillips left Tulane University in 1911 for a professorship at the University of Michigan. Neither Trent nor Bassett continued a major interest in southern history after transferring to the North; Phillips and Dodd accepted their calls with the avowed responsibility of writing and teaching the history of the South.

V

The southern avenue to the present has been advanced by the teaching of college and university courses in the history of the South, by the founding of the Southern Historical Association, by the establishment of university presses, and by the assembling of records in archives and libraries. Many developments in southern historical scholarship had their origins at Johns Hopkins University, the teaching of southern history among them. Students in "Adams' Seminary" investigated local institutions in the South and regional political and economic problems. An increasing clientele from the South led to series of lectures on that section. J. Franklin Jameson gave ten lectures on the political and constitutional history of the southern states in 1890–91, and David F. Houston, then of the University of Texas, lectured on the doctrine of nullification a decade later. Meanwhile, James C. Ballagh inaugurated the first systematic course in southern history in the spring semester of 1897–98. Described as southern economic history, it attracted eight graduate students. Ballagh's lectures were supplemented by weekly conferences. Either the lecture class or the weekly conference course, and sometimes both, was offered until 1903, but in the following decade he alternated courses on American slavery and secession. Among his students were Freeman and Eckenrode, who presented dissertations in southern history. Failure to replace Adams with a historian of equal stature and departure of Ballagh for the University of Pennsylvania in 1913 produced quiescence of southern history at Hopkins.

Loss of interest in the southern field at the Baltimore school was compensated for by Dunning at Columbia, the outpouring of southern doctors of philosophy continued unabated, and the teaching of the region's history found more recruits. By 1913 six institutions in the South were offering courses in southern history. The number increased to thirty or forty by the 1920's, most of them in the South, perhaps a half dozen north of the Ohio River. By 1940 about a hundred colleges and universities gave instruction in southern history. The great upsurge of interest was occasioned in part by the inauguration of the Southern Historical Association in 1934 and the founding of the *Journal of Southern History* the following year. Decreasing college enrollment during World War II resulted in abandonment of some of the offerings, but they were soon restored in the postwar period. While most of the interest still lies in the southern states, courses in the history of the South are available from Massachusetts to the Pacific Northwest.

Sensing the significance of this developing interest in southern history, reflected in courses and productive work, four historians in as many southern schools invited several scholars to assemble in Atlanta on November 2, 1934, to form a society devoted to the encouragement of teaching and research in the South. Before departing for the meeting, one of the founders pondered the problem of a scholarly periodical. No association of southern historians could hope to prosper unless it had a medium of publication. He therefore determined to sound out the administration at Louisiana State University on its willingness to sponsor a quarterly magazine devoted to southern history. After consulting the dean of the College of Arts and Sciences, a proposal to subsidize the organization in the amount of a thousand or fifteen hundred dollars was laid before the president. He liked the idea. Notwithstanding depression years, the university seemed to have plenty of money and an ambition for recognition in the scholarly world. He inquired how much money it would take to inaugurate a quarterly magazine of southern history. Fortunately, the interviewer hesitated a moment; and in the split second while he was contemplating whether to ask for the conservative figure of a thousand dollars or the unrealistic sum of fifteen hundred, the president said, "Well, speak up! Would five thousand dollars be enough?" The inquirer managed to stammer that with the exercise of rigid economy a reputable quarterly journal of history could be published with that amount. The generous subsidy enabled the Southern Historical Association to accumulate a balance of about nine thousand dollars before the *Journal of Southern History* left the university eight years later.

That the time was propitious for the organization of an association devoted mainly to southern history is evidenced by rapid growth in membership, well-attended annual meetings, genuine enthusiasm of the membership, and the early accumulation of a stockpile of acceptable articles and documents. The journal has not had to go begging for a home. When Louisiana State University relinquished the magazine at the end of 1942, Vanderbilt University readily accepted sponsorship; and after the journal had been published six years at that institution, the University of Kentucky enthusiastically accepted responsibility.

The work of the pioneers created a scholarly atmosphere that culminated in the association and its journal; a younger generation of historians merged harmoniously with a remnant of the older group to develop the southern field at quickened pace. Neophytes were inspired to organize courses in southern history, to inaugurate state historical society magazines or to revive decadent publications, to preserve historical records, to engage in research, to present papers at annual meetings. The twenty historians who assembled at Atlanta in 1934 performed a function which brought to significant climax an idea which the pioneers of 1900 dreamed of, but could not carry to fruition.

University presses have made an important contribution to the development of scholarship in the South by publishing many of the books that depict the history of the region. In earlier generations than the one under review, Southerners talked about the need for a great southern press to publish works by southern authors. Commercial conventions in the 1850's discussed the subject in connection with the publication of texts for use in southern schools. And as recently as the 1920's the spectre of provincialism was raised in exposés that advocated the establishment of a southern printing house to which Southerners could turn with confidence that creative and historical writing would reach the printed page. It is quite likely that such diatribes were prompted by the fact that northern publishers declined manuscripts that did not merit publication.

Northern university presses and commercial publishers have, as matter of fact, eagerly sought meritorious manuscripts about the South by southern authors. It could hardly be expected, however, that they could publish all the worthwhile studies, historical and otherwise, that came from southern writers. The University of North Carolina Press began its labors in the 1920's, and soon established an enviable reputation. By mid-twentieth century most of the southern state universities had established presses, and so had a few of the private schools. Their publications are a significant link in the raw material-researcher-publisher-reader chain.

The pioneers trained in the Adams and Dunning seminars were aware of an obligation to acquire raw materials as a first step in writing the history of the South, and several of them began collections that eventually became meccas for researchers. Manuscript collections are now as numerous as university presses. From Thomas M. Owen, who founded the Alabama State Department of Archives and History at the beginning of the century, to J. G. de Roulhac Hamilton, who devoted most of his time from 1930 forward to building up the Southern Historical Collection at the University of North Carolina, lies a story that would require many pages to relate. Also among the pioneers was Eugene C. Barker, who persuaded Colonel George W. Littlefield to subsidize a great Confederate Collection at the University of Texas. These and innumerable younger historians, librarians, and archivists merit acclaim for preserving the records of southern history.

VI

The teaching of southern history in colleges and universities posed the problem of a synthesis for classroom use. The first historians who gave attention to this problem were William K. Boyd of Trinity College and Robert P. Brooks of the University of Georgia, who compiled *A Selected Bibliography and Syllabus of the History of the South, 1584–1876,* for publication in 1918. Before the appearance of texts in southern history, beginning in the middle 1930's, some teachers used Phillips' *American Negro*

Slavery and *Life and Labor in the Old South* or volumes in the *Chronicles of America,* particularly Mary Johnson's *Pioneers of the Old South,* Constance L. Skinner's *Pioneers of the Old Southwest,* Jesse Macy's *Anti-Slavery Crusade,* Dodd's *Cotton Kingdom,* Fleming's *Sequel of Appomattox,* and Holland Thompson's *New South.*

Four textbooks in southern history have been published in the last twenty years. The first to appear was William B. Hesseltine's *A History of the South, 1607–1936* (1936), re-issued in a revised edition in 1943 under the more descriptive title *The South in American History.* This pioneer work had many commendatory qualities and served a useful purpose in guiding students through a previously uncharted course. Its design emphasized the South in the national picture. Robert S. Cotterill published a very brief *The Old South* (1936), with an entirely different concept of southern history, for he included only those events, institutions, and movements which were peculiarly southern. A third text appeared in 1947, *The South Old and New; A History, 1820–1947,* by Francis B. Simkins. He began his story with the 1820's, and the chapters on the Old South were too brief a discussion of the ante-bellum period for classes that devoted a semester to pre-Civil War history. This deficiency was corrected in a revised edition, *A History of the South* (1953), which carried the story back to the founding of the southern colonies. Clement Eaton's *A History of the Old South* (1951) gave fuller treatment of the ante-bellum period, emphasized the internal history of the section, and placed the South in the national framework.

A critical examination of writings in southern history from the pioneers to the present would make an appropriate summation of the section's historical scholarship, but the bulk of productivity precludes the task. The avenue to mid-century historiographic stature is lined with treatises great and small, competent and mediocre, set in closer proximity as the road approaches the present. A complete bibliography of works on the South, placed in critical perspective, would fill more than a massive volume; and an annotated compilation of important studies would yield a sizable book. The broad outlines of southern history are fairly well recognized; several significant themes have been competently treated; and many minutiae have been carefully examined. Time has dissipated most of the vestiges of sectional prejudice regardless of the authors' nativity or educational environment. The cumulative nature of knowledge has carried forward many of the pioneer's findings, with critical appraisal of evidence and conclusions; but the work of the last quarter century has been expansion more than correction. Scholars of the next generation need not fear that the avenue has reached its ultimate, for breadth is an inviting goal, depth a challenging ambition, and a new era's values a prompting stimulus.

CHAPTER TWO

William E. Dodd

Historian of Democracy

"MY LORD! Did you and I sleep in the same room in Crawfordsville! Well, well, well! Years from now they will put a brass tablet on that building on which will be inscribed these words: 'In this house the celebrated radical scholar, William E. Dodd, and the nefarious Scotch conservative and amateur biographer, Albert J. Beveridge, once slept, although on different nights.' . . . God help us all."

The biographer of John Marshall added this postscript in a letter to his Chicago critic about a year after the third and fourth volumes of the great work had been published. The two men had corresponded regularly since 1913, when Beveridge began serious investigation of the Chief Justice's career, and their exchanges continued through the Lincoln study. Their personal relations were cordial, but their historical concepts were antipodean, at least in Dodd's opinion. The point at issue, as he saw it, was property rights versus human rights, the interests versus the common man. Beveridge's insistence that Marshall's nationalism provided stability for the democracy of Thomas Jefferson, which was really "extreme individualism" rather than state rights, was an unacceptable thesis to the southern historian. "Your history is right so far as the facts go," he wrote Beveridge, "but wrong in so far as great causes of human action go." He credited the author with "deep and discriminating" knowledge, with amazing scholarship, and with "toilsome notes" which would serve him in teaching and in writing *his* "kind of a history of the period."

Dodd had already provided example of a different type of history, and he would write yet other books and articles that followed the same pattern of thought. His pages fairly bristle with English derivatives of *demokratia*. Whether he was writing about statesmen of the Old South or the new, the southern colonies in the seventeenth century or the United States in the nineteenth, or political and economic issues of the 1920's, the same democratic yardstick was applied to men, measures, and institutions.

But he was more than a passive historian of democracy and a biographer of democrats. "The only thing worth fighting for in this world is democracy," he wrote to his friend William K. Boyd. Like Jefferson, Lincoln, and Wilson, he had infinite faith in the common man, and like his prototypes he battled for the commoner's rights and liberties. He was an advocate as well as a historian of democracy. Humble origins and southern environment help to explain his elemental concepts.

I

Honest simplicity characterized the milieu into which Dodd was born four years after Appomattox. His birthplace was the vicinity of Clayton, North Carolina; his father, John Dodd, and his mother, Evelyn Creech, belonged to the undistinguished masses. Young Dodd attended Clayton High School, and he also studied at Oak Ridge Military Institute, where he achieved the highest academic rank. Meanwhile, in 1890, he had been an unsuccessful candidate for West Point. Despite the fact that eleven North Carolinians, including a sheriff, a clerk of court, two doctors, two state senators, and Josephus Daniels, endorsed his candidacy, the appointment went to another.

But their recommendation correctly emphasized enduring attributes. "Raised from a boy to manual labor," they wrote, "no service nor exposure can daunt him. Mentally he is apt, practical, ambitious, and determined." They also stressed his "conscientious sense of duty that leads him to be faithful to all his obligations."

In 1891 and again in 1893 Dodd passed teachers' examinations and received first grade certificates from the superintendents of Burke and Johnston counties. On one examination he rated perfect in English grammar. His poorest marks were in physiology and hygiene; in state and national history his scores were good. He served as principal of a private school in Glen Alpine, and during his college years he devoted summer vacations to teaching in private schools in Glen Alpine and Clayton.

From Oak Ridge Dodd transferred to Virginia Polytechnic Institute and graduated with distinction in 1895 with the B.S. degree. The general science curriculum was weighted heavily with mechanics, mathematics, and the sciences. Courses in English, Latin, French, and German emphasized grammar rather than humanistic learning and totaled less than a fourth of his program. The future professor of history and economics took one term of constitutional history and one of political economy, both of which were taught by Edward E. Sheib, doctoral graduate of the University of Leipzig. As extracurricular activities, Dodd edited the college magazine for three sessions, served as one of his society's debaters, won the essayist's medal, attained the rank of first lieutenant in the cadet corps, and, as president of the Y.M.C.A., attended the Northfield, Massachusetts, summer school. A prospective employer was assured a few years later that Dodd deported himself as "an active and consecrated Christian and Baptist," that he attended church and prayer meeting regularly, and that he taught a girls' class at Sunday school.

From 1895 to 1897 Dodd taught general history at V.P.I., and also earned the M.S. degree, which was awarded with honors. As a graduate student he studied French, German, and English literature. He escaped history entirely, but his knowledge of the subject was hardly as slight as the record indicates: Dodd's father recalled in 1933 that it had been "Will's hobby . . . since he was a boy."

It was not unusual in the closing years of the nineteenth century for young Americans to take their doctorates at German universities. With counsel from Professor Sheib and money borrowed from an uncle, Dodd went to the University of Leipzig in June, 1897, and continued there until November, 1899. Vacations were devoted to tours of Germany, France, Belgium, Switzerland, and England. His degree was awarded *magna cum laude,* although in history he graduated *summa cum laude.* Dodd's dissertation, *Jefferson's Rückkehr zur Politik, 1796,* was an unimpressive eighty-eight page treatise written in the German language. Among his professors was Erich Marcks, a Bismarck scholar who was still living when Dodd returned to Germany in 1933 as ambassador. The maestro at Leipzig was Karl Lamprecht. His *Deutsche Geschichte* depreciated political and church history, stressed economic and cultural segments, acclaimed collective society rather than the individual, and designated social psychology as the proper approach to the "science" of history.

Dodd returned to the United States saturated with Lamprecht, Niebuhr, Mommsen, and Ranke, but with little tangible background either for a study of southern history or for an interpretation of American democracy. He said in 1919 to Arthur W. Page that Lamprecht was "surely one of the greatest scholars in the world for facts," but he had given his American student no point of view. Dodd's interest in economic causation was in part derived from the German historian, but in this premise he was indebted fully as much to the influence of Charles A. Beard. His portraits of democratic leaders violated Lamprecht's insistence on genetic treatment of a whole society.

Although Dodd was unacquainted with Frederick Jackson Turner's "The Significance of the Frontier in American History" until the early years of his professorship at Randolph-Macon College, he was thereafter influenced more by the author's theories than by the writings of any other historian on either side of the Atlantic. Meanwhile, he had published *Nathaniel Macon,* begun in Leipzig and Göttingen and completed after his return to America. His research revealed "bitter rivalries of East and West" which "amounted almost to civil war at one time," but his biography of the North Carolinian was largely uninfluenced by "the greatest fact in our history." He might have continued "stumbling all about it" had he remained unaware of Turner's essay. "You see," he wrote to the Harvard professor, "historical writing is so conventional; men write from inherited points of view long after they think themselves wholly free; and in history, as in other lines of endeavor, men's minds are slow to see the whole significance of what they handle."

While Dodd conceded that Turner reshaped historical writing "more than any other man of his generation," he was no slavish disciple of the frontier historian. Their correspondence indicated concurrence on many basic interpretations of American history, divergence on others. As an example, Dodd believed that the nation was "a league of states" in the era of Jefferson Davis; Turner of course could not accept this thesis, which Dodd may have borrowed from Woodrow Wilson, who had already concluded that American nationality postdated the Civil War. Wilson's article, "A Calendar of Great Americans," suggested some interpretations to Dodd, but he could not accept Wilson's conclusion that Jefferson's Americanism was weakened by the influence of French philosophy. Perhaps Wilson's "Calendar" and William P. Trent's *Southern Statesmen of the Old Régime* provided Dodd with the idea for some of his own interpretive portraits of great Americans.

II

The months following Dodd's return to the United States were devoted to a search for employment and serious work on his Macon biography in the Library of Congress. When appointments at the University of Arkansas and Greenville Female College did not materialize, he sought a fellowship at Johns Hopkins University where he could attend classes in history and economics and continue his research. Herbert Baxter Adams could offer no encouragement either for a fellowship or for assistance in obtaining a position in one of the nearby boys' schools. Happily, in the fall of 1900, Dodd was appointed professor of history and economics at Randolph-Macon College with a salary of $700 and a teaching load of nine hours. Eventually he came to appreciate his assignment, but at the turn of the century it impressed him as a small Sahara rather than an intellectual oasis. Before the close of his second session he had sought positions at a dozen other institutions, some of which could have been no more desirable than the Ashland college. Perhaps Dodd can be forgiven his desire to abandon Randolph-Macon. Its resources, whether in faculty, students, library holdings, or income, were certainly small. The faculty, including the president, consisted of eight professors and six instructors. A library of 10,000 volumes and a student body of 150 supplied unimpressive statistics; a salary increase to $1,500 by his sixth year provided tangible evidence of administrative esteem for his services.

Dodd taught a variety of subjects, among them economics, civil government, "Present Politics," Western Europe, English history, the French Revolution and Napoleon, United States history, Virginia history, and the southern Confederacy. He persuaded historically minded Virginians to donate money for special library acquisitions, organized the Randolph-Macon Historical Society, assembled manuscripts from courthouses and private collections, and induced John P. Branch to subsidize an annual publication, the *Branch Historical Papers,* to which Dodd and his students contributed biographical sketches of early Virginians and selections from their correspondence. The historical writings of Dodd's students, and even some of his own editorial contributions, seem amateurish after the lapse of a half century, but the significance of his inspiring leadership transcends the intrinsic value of the end product. When one remembers that Dodd was in his thirties, that most of his students were undergraduates, and that historical scholarship in the South was in its infancy, his pioneering efforts assume their proper importance.

Assembling and preserving the raw materials of Virginia history became a major interest. "Much valuable material is going to ruin every day in Virginia for the lack of proper attention," he said in reporting a recent discovery. In ransacking a courthouse garret he uncovered a half-dozen large boxes of mouse-eaten deeds, wills, letters, and legal reports, some of them dating as far back as the late seventeenth century. The clerk of court "was astonished that he should be asked so minutely about such worthless stuff!" Dodd could not hope that Virginians would appreciate immediately the necessity for preserving private and official historical records, but the efforts of college teachers of history and their students would eventually contribute to that end. Each year his own neophytes, a few of them candidates for the master's degree, worked in local source materials, learned the fundamentals of research and writing, and through their articles and Dodd's own published documents an increasing number of Virginians came to understand the significance of historical records.

Dodd's success as a teacher, his participation in sessions devoted to southern history at annual meetings of the American Historical Association, his contributions to the *American Historical Review,* and the publication of *Nathaniel Macon* and *Jefferson Davis* brought him to the attention of scholars on other campuses. In 1908 he accepted a professorship at the University of Chicago which stipulated a beginning salary of $3,000, an eight-hour program in southern and western history, and $1,000 a year to spend for library acquisitions of southern materials. Before the position became permanent a year later, H. Morse Stephens offered strong inducements to attract Dodd to the University of California: a salary of $4,000, the ranking position in American history, the headship of the department after his own retirement, and a more delightful climate than Chicago afforded. Dodd consented to give a series of four lectures at Berkeley in the spring of 1909 on the general theme, the "Attempt of the South to Unite with [the] West for Imperial Purposes before the Civil War," with specific lectures on Henry Clay, John C. Calhoun, Stephen A. Douglas, and Jefferson Davis. A week in California convinced Dodd that he should continue in Chicago despite the weather. He cited as reasons for his decision Berkeley's remoteness from the South, the opportunity to build up a regional collection at Chicago, the pleasure of working with southern students, and a liberal teaching arrangement which provided four months annual leave.

III

The quarter century of Dodd's tenure at the University of Chicago witnessed some notable achievements, whether as collector, teacher, lecturer, or author. His most significant accomplishment in adding research materials to the library was the acquisition in 1913 of the Colonel Reuben T. Durrett Collection of Kentuckiana, Virginiana, newspaper and periodical files, pamphlets and prints, maps and government documents which provided research topics for sundry graduate students. Purchased for $25,000 after a year of negotiations with the Louisville family, the collection strengthened materially the library's holdings of both manuscript and printed sources in southern history.

Dodd's call to the University of Chicago contemplated courses in western as well as southern history; actually, his teaching was confined almost exclusively to the history of the South. His predecessors, J. Franklin Jameson and Edwin E. Sparks, had brought their offerings to the periphery of that field. Dodd was the first, and for a long time the only, historian in any college or university who devoted all of his time to courses in southern history. Occasionally he surveyed the region's social, economic, and political history from the founding of Jamestown to the twentieth century; more often he concentrated on some period or segment, particularly of the lower South. Secession, the Confederacy, and Reconstruction appeared frequently as seminar subjects. Southern influence in the Old Northwest illustrated his interest in the impact of his native region on that in which he lived. A recital of catalogue listings should be qualified, however, by the observations that variation in title did not necessarily mean a proportionate change in subject matter and that seminar students were not required to choose topics which fell within the scope of course descriptions.

Publications were important in establishing Dodd's reputation as a historian of the South, but his greatest contribution to scholarship was his inspirational teaching. Enrollment remained relatively small until after World War

I, but during his last fifteen years at Chicago the number of students in his classes increased appreciably. Before leaving the university for Berlin he took inventory of his services to doctoral candidates: fifty had written their dissertations under his direction. In seminars as in thesis guidance, independent work was encouraged by a minimum of direct instruction and a maximum of individual initiative. As a classroom lecturer Dodd had a strange capacity to mold the mind with hypnotic effect. He dispensed with the formidable barricade of such technicalities as periodic quizzes and long reading lists and evaluated final examinations and term reports with dishonest generosity. Some students worked hard; others learned much even though they contributed little to self-improvement. His lectures were interpretive and impressionistic rather than informative and narrative. Classes were intellectual experiences from which students profited even though the instructor was "incredibly easy." The source of Dodd's power as a stimulating teacher, wrote one student whose "intellectual outlook had been *remade*," was "the impact of a unique personality coming through every external obstacle."

Another student who attained distinction in his own right and who succeeded to the position Dodd vacated in 1933 summarized his qualities as "a great teacher": "Something about the personality, something about the method, awakened interest in what he taught and inspired independent effort in the field. About him was the graciousness, the quaintness, and the pathos of the South from which he came. He had its quality of always being personal, even in public lectures, and with it the rare gift of always including others in the conversation even when he did all the talking. He had a way of making others think that they were equally responsible for the thoughts which he alone supplied. . . . Students, who only listened believed themselves admitted into the companionship of the scholar, and

felt the thrill of sharing in the discovery of new facts and
new interpretations. His lectures were informal, sometimes
interspersed with comments or questions directed at some
individual who was not necessarily expected to reply but
who, by inference, was given credit for knowing all the answers whether he did or not. . . . Students flocked about
him and hung on his words, quoted him on all occasions,
and rose in quick defense at the slightest suggestion of
criticism. . . . Imaginations were stimulated. Interest was
stirred not only by a past that lived, but by a teaching personality which seemed to grip the present firmly because
it knew the past. Here was something unexplainably practical. . . . The urge to scholarship was unmistakable.
Even the desire to help save democracy was not absent."

IV

As a productive scholar Dodd's quantitative record was
notable. In a period of four decades he wrote eight volumes
of biography and history, collaborated in the editing of
six others, and published scores of articles and reviews in
professional journals, weekly magazines, and newspapers.
Four of these years—the period of his diplomatic service
in Berlin—were all but lost to scholarship, summer sojourns at his Virginia farm were interludes of academic
quiescence, and lecture tours during the fifteen years prior
to his departure for Germany retarded productivity.

Evaluating his books at mid-century, only one of them
has stood the test of time. If this sweeping verdict seems
too depreciatory, it should be understood that few books
survive the generation in which they are written, and that
Dodd's contemporaries, including college students, read
some of his with avid interest. Correspondents penned their
appreciations, reviewers commended meritorious qualities.

They also discovered errors of fact and untenable conclusions.

Of the three biographies, *Nathaniel Macon, Jefferson Davis,* and *Woodrow Wilson and His Work,* only the first has not been superseded, for until recently no other scholar has elected to investigate Macon's career. Dodd's biography was concerned more with the political history of the period from Washington to Jackson than with Macon himself. A paucity of manuscripts, limited use of printed sources, and chief reliance upon James Schouler's *History of the United States* gave it undefinitive repute. *Jefferson Davis* marked an advancement toward historical maturity, whether in research or craftsmanship, but the author ignored many available sources and nearly forgot the chief character once he was elected president of the Confederacy. *Woodrow Wilson,* too contemporary for perspective and too personal for objectivity, has only historiographical value thirty-five years after publication.

Dodd had considerable genius in interpretive portraiture, and two of his books fell into this category. No one would consult *Statesmen of the Old South* today for an interpretation of Calhoun or Davis, and yet Dodd's analysis of the metamorphosis of the Jeffersonian party from radicalism in the revolutionary generation, through conservatism under the leadership of Calhoun, to domination by property rights in the era of Jefferson Davis still makes sense. The portrait of Jefferson, his most significant achievement, can still be read with profit. No one can understand Dodd the historian or Dodd the democratic personality without comprehending the work's underlying philosophy. When the author designated the book as his "article of faith," he had special reference to the Jefferson chapter. *Lincoln or Lee* faded faster than *Statesmen of the Old South,* for words and phrases seemed more important to Dodd in 1927 than ideas and concepts. As popular lectures to university audiences, the three essays made alluring appeal, but the printed sentences remind the reader of series of after-thoughts strung together on tenuous lines of familiar events, and a plethora of adjectives—hazardous words for the precisionist—accompanies the introduction of rivals and partisans.

Three of Dodd's books were histories. *Expansion and Conflict,* adequate in its day, has gone the way of other handbooks designed primarily for classroom use. His most widely read book was his contribution to the *Chronicles of America* Series, *The Cotton Kingdom,* characterized by Carl Becker as "a masterly little sketch of a big subject." Despite the title, it was little concerned with the kingdom of cotton. Evidence of haste in writing appears in the volume as well as in the author's diary and correspondence. On one occasion he noted that it was written in two months; on another, in six weeks. *The Old South; Struggles for Democracy* was marred in the making. The potter lost enthusiasm for his ware in the quarter century that elapsed between the design and the completed vessel. Seventeenth-century history was unfamiliar terrain, and the writer found more examples of democracy than the evidence warranted. The first volume of the unfinished work did not fulfill its promise.

The significance of Dodd's books does not lie in any great contribution to knowledge, for he did not delve deeply nor exhaustively into the raw materials of history. It cannot be said that he became a final authority on any subject he investigated. A high incidence of error characterized his work. He never mastered the art of documentation: his footnotes are often bewildering in form and purpose.

Despite paucity of investigation and lack of precision,

Dodd's contributions were nonetheless real. As a historian of the South he helped to inaugurate scholarly treatment of the region's past. He was a pioneer in presenting the tripartite sectionalism of the ante-bellum period. In treating the wellsprings of human action, he found a plausible explanation in economic factors. The American democratic tradition assumed new significance as a rationale of sectional controversy and the human equation. His philosophy of the tradition was pragmatic, expressed always in unphilosophic phrase. Dodd was not given to speculative thought.

Northern historians were impressed with his dispassionate treatment of southern subjects. Charles Francis Adams, in reviewing *Jefferson Davis* for the *American Historical Review,* credited the author with "two great essentials" of the biographer: "He is thoroughly sympathetic with his subject; and yet throughout judicial in tone." His "critical attitude," the reviewer discovered, had "excited more or less adverse comment in what was once the Confederacy." After reading *Statesmen of the Old South,* Turner wrote the author that "the whole book is a bully corrective to the traditional treatment." This appraisal must have pleased Dodd exceedingly. "The purpose of my studying and writing history," he wrote to Theodore Roosevelt, "is to strike the balance somewhat between the North and the South, but not to offer any defense of any thing." His great problem, he continued, was to convince "the conservative South and the now reactionary East" that this method was historical; both feared "the logic of the thing so much that the premises must be denied even when self-evident." It did not disturb him that Confederate veterans in Virginia and Union soldiers in Chicago protested his preachments. Only once did he struggle with his conscience in weighing evidence: the contemporaneity of Wilson's war career and his own interest in the success of the Democratic party led him to compromise between his obligations to Clio and Demos.

In his efforts to discover the causes of human action, Dodd recognized an ageless clash between property rights and human rights, which he equated in terms of monopolistic interests and the common man. Political behavior was explainable, he thought, only if projected against a background of economic history. Yet he was no economic determinist: "The history of the United States must be rewritten from start to finish," he said in 1916, "not with a view to economic determinism . . . but with full appreciation of economic factors. By appreciation I mean actual use of these factors in the warp and woof of written history."

V

In presenting democracy historically or in advocating it for his own generation, Dodd was fully aware that undemocratic groups prevented a fair trial of his political, economic, and social concept. Plantation barons of the antebellum South and industrial magnates of the twentieth century—each monopolists in their own day—stood athwart the realization of his ideal.

As early as 1907 he pointed to the similarity between the two groups. His *Jefferson Davis* analyzed the monopolists of the last ante-bellum decade. Allied with great plantation lords of the Charleston-Beaufort and Mississippi Delta regions were the less opulent black-belt planters from Washington to New Orleans, for "the charmed circle of Southern aristocracy" was not closed to ambitious men of moderate wealth. All subscribed to the fetish of state rights. A twentieth of the population, inhabiting a tenth of the southern area, constituted a "monopolistic class" which dominated political action.

The geographical location and functional economy of the monopolists shifted during the next half century to the Northeast. By 1906 "the lords of industry and transportation" were "as loth to surrender any of their monopoly rights as were those of 1861." Untrammeled by federal authority "and licensed by the individual states," twentieth-century industrialists worked their "will on the people." Dodd advanced the view that there was "as much slavery connected with the later as with the earlier system, and far more hardship and suffering." Amplifying his position to a reviewer, he explained: "Indeed I do not remember to have said the ills of our industrialism are 'worse' than those of slavery. I ought to have said as bad as those of slavery— that is my opinion." "Have you not observed," he inquired of Charles Francis Adams, "how nearly like our great slave masters of 1830–1860 are our present industrial and transportation lords?" Jefferson Davis, ante-bellum "champion of vested rights," was no more guilty of "treason in the extreme demands of privilege in 1861" than the northern senator of a half century later who defied the power of national authority to pass regulatory railroad laws.

This analogy was stated in nearly the same terms in *Statesmen of the Old South:* All powers of southern state governments, whether executive, legislative, or judicial, "were in the hands of men who owned slaves just as all these functions of most of the Northern and Eastern states today are dominated by the corporations and the monopolistic interests." By the time he published *Expansion and Conflict* in 1915, he was ready to assign millowners of the Northeast an ante-bellum role comparable to contemporary southern planters. Occupying a relatively small area, "these able and prosperous makers of a new era in the East" worked "their two million operatives" fully as long and as hard as planters did their slaves.

What strange shifts in attitude toward slavery two generations had wrought! At a dinner party given by the Dodds in Harry P. Judson's honor in 1916, the president of the University of Chicago remarked "that slavery was the only proper way to manage and work the negroes of the Old South." This was indeed "strange doctrine from one who served a year in . . . the war to exterminate slavery!" Judson had expressed the view many times before, Dodd recorded, and so had other people he had met in Chicago and elsewhere in the North. Capital's labor problem, Dodd was convinced, "brought so many people to this view." Had northern employers finally accepted the extreme preachments of George Fitzhugh, propagandist of the Old South, who pointed to the advantages of slave labor over free and advocated the extension of the Old South's benevolent system to England and the North?

Dodd would have answered that question with a decided negative, for it involved an erroneous premise: slavery was not a benevolent system. In the twentieth century, as in the eighteenth, it violated the philosophy of Jefferson's democratic manifesto of 1776. "There can be no political democracy where economic democracy fails," Dodd said in explaining the failure of the second Cleveland administration. Decay had begun, however, two generations before Grover Cleveland cast his lot with the moneyed interests. In fact, social democracy as well as political and economic democracy disintegrated as the doctrines of the Declaration of Independence receded into the past. "In New England, as in the South, democracy was flouted and a privileged position greatly prized." It made no difference that one was an urban and the other a rural aristocracy.

Despite a modicum of truth in this oversimplified analogy, the fallacies are readily apparent. The social structure of the ante-bellum South was not so unhealthy as Dodd would have us believe, and the plain folk were more articulate politically than "planter domination" suggests. Per-

haps some northern industrialists and transportation magnates looked with nostalgic eyes upon an ante-bellum labor
system which, in romantic literature at least, stood in sharp
contrast with twentieth-century demands for reform. Dodd's
democratic philosophy made the one labor system as impossible as the other. Yet the analogy was an effective device
in correcting the historical imbalance between the North
and the South, and perhaps that was the historian's chief
reason for reiterating it.

VI

In recording America's past Dodd made no effort to
conceal his sympathy for the common man nor his confidence that practical democracy, if given a fair trial, would
exalt his social, economic, and political station. As historian and biographer he would therefore emphasize that
concept which provided a means to the proper end. Occasionally, statesmen of the Federalist-Whig school, as
Marshall and Henry Clay, diverted his attention; but the
men in whose careers he reveled were Jeffersonian Republicans and Democrats—Jefferson himself, Spencer Roane,
John Taylor, Nathaniel Macon, Thomas Ritchie, John
C. Calhoun, Jefferson Davis, and Woodrow Wilson. Abraham Lincoln, Republican, qualified for Dodd's democratic
honor roll better than any of the others. Jackson, Tilden,
and Cleveland sometimes aroused his enthusiasm, but they,
like Calhoun and Davis, lacked many of the attributes of
the true democrat. The men who best illustrated Dodd's
concept of democracy were Jefferson, Lincoln, and Wilson,
and these names occur repeatedly in his writings and correspondence.

Thomas Jefferson, peasant planter, aristocratic leveler,
religious liberal, educated politician, advocate of democracy, symbol of the first American West, "political saint to

Abraham Lincoln"; Jefferson, "with a boundless faith in the masses." Abraham Lincoln, personification of the log cabin, friend of the common man and a common man himself, symbol of the westward-moving frontier, religious free-thinker, discerning judge of human nature, amiable philosopher, advocate of the great Declaration's egalitarian pronunciamento, "political saint to Woodrow Wilson"; Lincoln, with an implicit faith in the common man. Woodrow Wilson, humanitarian, descendant of Scotch peasants, symbol of the aristocracy of learning, "a great passionate human figure . . . convinced of its mission," heir of Lincoln more than of Jefferson, "the most consummate master of convincing statement," Lincoln only excepted; Wilson, "a second Jefferson, or better, perhaps, a second Lincoln." These are the attributes of America's greatest champions of democracy—as Dodd understood them.

Of Jefferson and Lincoln, Dodd sometimes wrote with alarming assurance; of Wilson he was less certain. He admitted that the war President "presents some difficulties." The author of *Woodrow Wilson and His Work* was a Democrat in politics; he was also a democrat in his social philosophy. The subject of his biography was "a Democrat and *almost* a democrat." The distinction bears repeating. The President was "almost" the democrat in social philosophy Dodd hoped he would be. But not quite. Dodd's democracy had exacting qualifications. Unfortunately, Wilson was a paradox. Occasionally he seemed "too much a man of this world, too nearly a representative of the old order to make his calling and election with men like Jefferson and Lincoln sure." Later chapters of the book show that the biographer was "struggling with this contradiction in him." Dodd "would have him simply a folks man and nothing else."

The biographer was not only mildly disappointed in his idol, he was also apprehensive of the drift toward totalitarianism. His depressed spirit emerges between the lines of *Woodrow Wilson,* especially those which record the war and treaty years. His faith in democracy received rude shocks as Theodore Roosevelt and Leonard Wood preached universal military training, as the United States risked preservation of her own democracy by entering a war to preserve it in other lands, as the interests conspired to defeat Wilson's idealistic peace and the League of Nations.

But if Dodd questioned Wilson's loyalty to his faith and democracy's prospects for the future, others doubted the soundness of the biographer's analysis of the President and his problems. Houghton Mifflin and Macmillan declined the manuscript. To Macmillan critics who spoke of the author's "partisan view," the biographer made a spirited reply. Two eastern elements would of course regard his work as partisan: "the older social groups" whose traditions were Republican and whose antecedents were protariff; and "the younger radical groups" whose advocacy of "a proletarian dictatorship" would result in a regime as undemocratic as that which terminated with Taft's defeat in 1912. The author's sectional prejudice came to the surface in explaining the East's rejection of the presidential program. In submitting the manuscript to Arthur W. Page he complained of the indifference of Boston and New York periodicals to Wilson. Such indifference was natural, he wrote, for no great American leader could represent the East or satisfy its journals. The section itself had produced no great American leaders. Washington, Hamilton, and Adams were great leaders, but they were Europeans. Benjamin Franklin, despite Philadelphia residence, was actually a spokesman of western Pennsylvanians. "Jefferson and Jackson and Lincoln were great American leaders," but they sprang from "the mass of common and provincial folk." Easterners, he said, "may put out the news, publish the literature and finance everything; but they cannot be immortal."

Page could follow Dodd a part of the way, but he could not accept his entire portrait. "I believe that to a considerable degree your picture of the virtuous Americanism of the West and South and the unrighteous industrialism of the East is correct," but these contrasts were etched in too bold relief. The whole West was "not purely American," and Page had observed more disapproval of "*rural* degradation" and industrial abuses in New York than in his native state of North Carolina. Eastern "sophisticated intellectuals . . . of whom Wilson himself was a member" had initiated income tax, civil service, and other reforms. Dodd replied that he was "no propagandist"; his conclusions pained his soul, for the United States was "upon a steady and irresistible drift away from democracy." He admitted that the behavior of agriculturists and industrialists was essentially the same. Exploitation, whether by industry or agriculture, made democracy seem illusive. But he was sure that the "present industrial civilization is irrevocably headed to a sort of feudalism that must cover the earth."

VII

An increasing emphasis on advocacy of democracy beginning with World War I diminished Dodd's opportunity to make enduring contributions as a research scholar. He sacrificed formal history for the more ephemeral current issues that he discussed in newspaper and magazine articles and in scores of lectures. His correspondence with Democratic politicians increased, he took a lively interest in political campaigns, and now and then he pondered whether he should seek political office. Never an "ivory tower" historian, he became a public citizen, a man with a mission. He could speak authoritatively on the democratic tradition in American life, and that tradition was in greater danger than in any preceding generation. Who was better prepared than a historian of democracy to advocate its continuation in a period of domestic and international crisis?

Dodd's interest in practical politics and public affairs that culminated in his appointment as ambassador to Germany in 1933 began more than a quarter of a century earlier. He ventilated his views when politicos violated his idealistic concept of government; he consciously sought contacts with influential public figures. Historians are seldom invited to the White House; Dodd was an exception, for two presidents received him cordially at the executive mansion. The fact that Theodore Roosevelt and Woodrow Wilson were members of the historical guild aided *entrée.*

The earliest glimpse of Dodd as a militant citizen dates back to his years as professor at Randolph-Macon College. He battled against Virginia's Democratic machine headed by Thomas F. Ryan, corresponded with William Jennings Bryan on issues of the 1908 campaign, supplied the Democratic press bureau with campaign data, and voted for the Nebraskan because a few more Republican administrations would endanger the American way of life and work. He favored breaking the solid South "in a noble cause," but he would not "help a party which cries 'wolf' every four years and then kicks the rescuer down the back stairs."

An inscribed copy of *Jefferson Davis* brought the author an invitation to dine with President Roosevelt to "talk over some of the points" raised by the biography. The invitation was "equal to a command," and the relatively obscure historian from the other side of Mason and Dixon's line reveled in distinguished company for an hour and a half. Among the guests were Ambassador and Lady Bryce, Lyman Abbott, two congressmen, and a governor. Dodd was seated next to Bryce, with whom he discussed Jeremy Bentham and *The American Commonwealth*. Soon the conversation turned to the Confederate president's new portrait, which Roosevelt "said was very valuable and especially well-done." Many years before he had said some critical things about Davis in a *Century* article which he would now like to retract. In a rare mood of modesty, Roosevelt promised a history that would correct all of his errors; in fact, when he considered his mistakes, historical and otherwise, he marveled that he was President. Dodd's comment approached sycophancy: "It is just because of what you have said, Mr. President, and what you have done that you are President." Three weeks later the historian wrote a long memorandum of his thrilling adventure. He spoke of Roosevelt's active intellect, sharp perception, frank discussion of "delicate subjects," willingness to acknowledge error, and defense of his convictions. The "blunt, quick and outspoken" President contrasted sharply with the quiet, cautious, and reserved Bryce. Lyman Abbott, *Outlook* editor, was "liberal toward Southern men and history"; Roosevelt even more so. Dodd's sober afterthoughts were less generous. Several years later he recalled that Roosevelt unconsciously sought to convince his visitor that he should abandon his Democracy for Republicanism. After the United States entered World War I the New Yorker became a "braggart and demagogue" incapable of performing his proper duty in the military crisis.

A few campaign speeches for Wilson in 1912 led Dodd to believe that he was sufficiently inside the party to propose for the President's consideration the establishment of a great national weekly to "interpret faithfully and attractively" administrative policies and measures. An "unofficial censorship," he said, prevented free discussion of great industrial combinations and department stores except in independent and radical papers. Such an "educative" weekly, free of politics "in the meaner sense," would create "an intelligent public opinion." Failure of the newspaper to materialize did not diminish Dodd's interest in the success of the administration nor his advocacy of Wilson's re-election. As the United States drifted toward war, he called at the White House to present "a mild protest," endorsed by some of his Chicago colleagues, against the spread of militarism. Wilson received his complaint sympathetically, explained his determination to avoid martyrdom for Leonard Wood, and stressed his own policy of developing sufficient strength for preservation of peace. A striking parallel "between the present ruler of the nation and the rough man of 1861" impressed Dodd, who decided that Wilson was "an aristocratic democrat if that be possible," a statesman as well as a politician, prime minister as well as President.

The interview may have inspired Dodd to write a biography of Wilson. Two years later he dined at the White House to acquire personal data. The President's blessing was "reverend and dignified"; the luncheon no more elaborate than a fifty-cent meal at the Cosmos Club. As Wilson escorted Dodd to the study, the President talked about "the strong religious atmosphere in which he grew up," the advantage of being "brought up poor," the failure of Germans to understand the American common man because their Christianity was only a veneer, the fearful responsibility of "executive supremacy" in American government. Dodd devoted thirty pages in his diary to the three-hour interview. Wilson "is a very great man," he mused after pondering the President's frank and fearless words.

The historian made scores of speeches on Wilson and the League in postwar years, and he also wrote articles for newspapers and periodicals on these subjects and the farm problem. Such themes brought his name conspicuously to the attention of Democratic leaders. The party's 1920 candidate, James M. Cox, sent him an advance copy of the speech of acceptance, requesting assistance on the League of Nations segment. Dodd rewarded Cox with a copy of

Woodrow Wilson and His Work and the observation that the acceptance speech was "every thing a progressive-minded person could wish." He kept a foot in the Democratic doorway by attending open sessions of the National Committee's St. Louis meeting in 1921. Election of Cordell Hull, friend of William G. McAdoo, to the chairmanship pleased Dodd exceedingly, and so did the decided Wilson sentiment manifested by the committee. If Wilson did not recover, McAdoo might be the 1924 nominee, or perhaps "young Roosevelt," which "would not be bad."

Apparently the Democratic label was more important to Dodd than consistency in political principles. How an independent thinker could labor for McAdoo in the pre-convention campaign, endorse John W. Davis as a man who would "make one of the great presidents," and enthuse over Alfred E. Smith for 1928 is beyond comprehension, but Dodd negotiated all the hurdles. In 1924 "a wet ticket or a Catholic" would be suicidal; but a year later, fore-seeing the "Happy Warrior's" nomination, he rationalized the dilemma to Josephus Daniels. He preferred a wet Catholic and alienation of the South to a continuation in power of the big business element with its "economic imperialism." He was not surprised that Daniel C. Roper disagreed with him. But, he pointed out, the twenty million well-organized Catholics had great political strength, and besides, they were laborers, "the poor of the North." The Republicans, controlled by a financial and business hierarchy that would continue to promote "American feudalism," were Protestant only "in the mere matter of form." The South was also "Protestant, but not deeply religious"; it was also "Democratic, but not much more Democratic than religious." Why worry about a nomination that would alienate the region of Roper's and Dodd's nativity?

Dodd could exult in the Democratic victory of 1932, especially when it was rumored that the Roosevelt ad-

ministration might need his services. He lunched with
Roper and several other loyal party workers in Washington
on March 15. Already, before the inauguration, a long-
distance call had inquired whether Dodd's services would
be available, but he replied "that there was no position
for which . . . [he was] properly equipped." He might,
however, give part time to the government if he "could
render service, without seeming to be a grafter on the
public . . . though I believe my history might never appear," which would mean "failure in life." The Berlin post
was offered, and Dodd accepted it. Only one volume of the
Old South history was completed, but procrastination and
its ally ill health were already assuring a fragment.

VIII

Some academicians have pursued farming as an avoca-
tion, prompted perhaps by the Jeffersonian tradition rather
than any genuine love for the soil. Dodd, like Jefferson,
held rural democracy in high esteem, but it would be a mistake to conclude that a primary motive in his decision to
buy a Virginia farm was the agrarian example of his
eighteenth-century prototype. Unlike the Nashville agrar-
ians of the 1920's, Dodd was no traditionalist; his own
bucolic adventure was a means of preserving health. Never
a robust man, he was increasingly plagued by nervous indigestion and headaches, and his sojourns in the Old Dominion provided escape from the complex role of teacher,
researcher, lecturer, and diplomat. His months at Round
Hill illustrated rather than promoted his democratic philosophy. The mold into which it was cast emanated from his
Carolina boyhood.

A few years after he moved to Chicago, Dodd purchased
a ninety-acre farm in Loudoun County, Virginia, and ere
long he had invested $15,000 in the enterprise. In the fall

of 1914 he informed his friend Boyd that he was "so absorbed in making things grow" that he could "not discuss even so interesting a subject as history intelligently." Despite some success in producing grain and milk and peaches, farm life was no utopia. It "serves to set me up physically each year," he recorded in his diary, "but it also tries my spirit very often."

What tried his spirit most was the attitude of neighbors, tenants, and laborers who sought to profit from his inexperience, but this situation had changed by 1919. "Jeered at as a 'book farmer' when I began, I have now the honor to be respected by the hard and closefisted farmers of the county. Nobody calls me 'professor'; but plain Mr. Dodd and I am treated as an equal." More significant than small dividends that could be measured in dollars and cents, his "vacations proved to be tonics," better than his Chicago doctors could prescribe. After four years he "could do more literary work and teach with more vigor than any of . . . [his] colleagues. That was the first result and the most important. That is what every intellectual needs to know. . . . Men need to work with their hands."

Farmer Dodd appreciated his self-admonition even when he was powerless to observe it. The strain and tension of his diplomatic responsibilities in Germany accelerated spells of indigestion and headache. In the spring of 1936 he was permitted six weeks at Round Hill, the happiest of his postacademic career. He led a less vigorous life, for no longer could he plow and plant, but he spent ten hours a day out of doors, assisting and supervising his workmen in improvements and repairs. He noted in his diary, "There were people who seemed amazed that I should work with ordinary laborers." Whether historian, farmer, or diplomat, he personified democracy.

Dodd's democratic way of living continued through his years as ambassador to Germany, exhibited now and then in affectation of a cherished role. He succeeded in maintaining the Berlin post on his salary, and he insisted that diplomatic and consular representatives of the United States should live within their incomes. He complained to the State Department that two-member families of the diplomatic corps "shipped furniture enough for twenty-room houses at the cost of $3,000." One of his own assistants in Berlin employed a valet, a butler, a porter, a chauffeur, two maids, and two cooks. He angered a member of his staff who frequently sent hundred-dollar telegrams by insisting that they should be briefer. Extravagance with government money and polite hours were characteristic of diplomatic employees. Graduates of Harvard and Princeton, they were "sons of rich men, hardly one in ten has ever learned anything about clear-cut, succinct writing, even less about history." These ill-informed snobs were "bent upon exploiting the Foreign Service for their set."

It was even more shocking to find European countries that could not pay their war debts to the United States maintaining expensive establishments in Berlin. The Italian ambassador, Vittorio Cerruti, occupied a "palace," and "servants attired in 18th century livery" reminded Dodd of the age of Louis XV. An elaborate dinner given by the Italian was a "show" that probably cost $800. Later the same evening the Dodds attended the German Foreign Minister's reception of seven hundred guests at the Hotel Kaiserhof. "It was a grand show that must have cost more than $1,000, at the expense of poor Germany!" Dodd may have been posing when he showed his contempt for such display by recording that he ate a stewed peach and drank a glass of milk before retiring.

Contrasting with the lavishness of Italian, Rumanian, and Belgian dinners, the American ambassador entertained a score of diplomats at a cost of one or two hundred dollars. His butler Fritz embarrassed him by packing his suitcases for a trip; Dodd did "not think it a disgrace for a man to pack his own bags." But Dodd in turn embarrassed a hotel butler who had followed the ambassador to help him into his car. "He was astonished, perhaps disgusted, when he saw me *walk* off briskly toward the Embassy." If the diplomat traveled by train, he went second or third class; and it was only after his Chevrolet was wrecked that he appeased protocol by buying a Buick.

Was Dodd genuinely sincere in these outward manifestations of the democratic spirit? In his formative years an atmosphere of austerity prohibited a habit of play and the development of an esthetic sense. Hence he seldom engaged in any activity for pure enjoyment, nor did he cultivate a taste for the arts. Associates with social graces made him ill at ease. He had little experience in sharing the passions and pleasures and prejudices of plain people, although a sixth sense enabled him—through the medium of historical documents—to understand their struggles for human rights and their contributions to civilization. Separateness created insecurity, and insecurity accentuated the natural trait of democratic simplicity to conceal social deficiencies. As Dodd acquired stature as a historian and recognition as a public citizen, the characteristic overshadowed its origins. Benjamin Franklin played peasant in Paris with considerable charm. Peasantry procreated a democratic tradition, and Dodd endeavored to personify it in Berlin, though with less success. He may have had posterity in mind as he wrote in his diary of expensive drinks and dinners and of his own preference for milk and stewed peaches—dietary necessities rather than symbols of Jeffersonian simplicity. But the trait was basically genuine, and its possessor would have been less than human if he had not added a bit of posing to his preaching.

What was the measure of the man who wore the democratic tradition so visibly? A dynamic teacher who inspired his students, a writer who united past and present in a stream of history that made both intelligible, a citizen who recognized an obligation to enlighten society, a public servant who faithfully performed his duties—these were outward manifestations of solid worth. But the man himself was greater than his works, for he was a symbol of those qualities which middle-class Americans have come to look upon as a heritage. The closing sentence of his *Nathaniel Macon* is equally applicable to the biographer: *"He actually believed in democracy."*

CHAPTER THREE

Ulrich B. Phillips
Historian of Aristocracy

"SOUTHERN HISTORY is almost a virgin field, and one of the richest in the world for results. The history of the United States has been written by Boston, and largely written wrong. It must be written anew before it reaches its final form of truth. And for that work . . . the South must do its part in preparation. New England has already overdone its part. There have been antiquarians and chroniclers at work in the Southern field, but few historians —few thinkers—and thought is the all-essential. I have only begun to dabble in the edge of it; but the results are already quite surprising. A study of the conditions of the Old South from the inside readily shows an immense number of errors of interpretation by the old school of historians. . . . What must be sought is the absolute truth, whether creditable or not. My lectures on the history of slavery, with an economic interpretation; on the plantation system; and on political parties and doctrines in the South, are received as little short of revelations by men who have thought that they knew American history. I am not rushing these things into print, because it is necessary to study them further to guard against errors of fact or interpretation."

When Ulrich B. Phillips penned this analysis of a problem and his ambition to contribute a solution, he was a youthful instructor of twenty-six at the University of Wisconsin, just out of his doctorate at Columbia. At the moment he was concerned with a movement to invigorate

the state historical society of his native Georgia; but under-
neath wise counsel to reformers in Savannah lay a deep
conviction that history had dealt unjustly, through neglect
and distortion, with the southern region. Where exor-
dium existed, he would amplify; where misconception prevailed, he would revise. Other scholars native and adopted
accepted the same responsibilities, but no historian of the
first third of the twentieth century contributed so large a
measure of expansion and revision. His thirty-two productive years yielded some forty-eight hundred printed
pages, most of them relating to the Old South. His writings
were significant, but he suffered the usual fate of revisionists, for some of his conclusions wore an impress of southern
tradition. Thanks to his poised and prolific pen, the pen-
dulum was nearer equilibrium in 1934 than it had been
at the turn of the century.

I

If Phillips' memory served him well in 1926, and mine
has not erred in the interim, two books stimulated his
interest in the South's history; two others prompted a belief
that northern historians perverted it. Before entering the
University of Georgia he read Susan Dabney Smedes'
idyllic memoir of her father, *Memorials of a Southern
Planter,* and Daniel R. Hundley's *Social Relations in Our
Southern States,* an able analysis of classes in ante-bellum
society that refuted partisans from another section with a
show of surface irritation. As an undergraduate at the university he studied the early volumes of James Ford Rhodes
and John Bach McMaster. A chapter on slavery in the first
volume of the *History of the United States from the Compromise of 1850* was a strange medley of truth, half-truth,
and error, of uncritical use of prejudiced sources and
reliance upon valid evidence, of generous understanding

of the South's problems and wholesale repudiation of her means of solving them. McMaster's presentation of slavery in his *History of the People of the United States* differed only in degree; perhaps he wore his irritation just as visibly. These works, whether by northern or southern writers, seemed unreal to the young Georgian who had already developed the habit of thought, and they stirred a desire to search for the truth. Did it not lie somewhere between southern romanticism and northern nescience?

Born in 1877, Phillips was a product of the Old South as well as the new. The year marked the technical end of Reconstruction, for home rule was restored a few months before his birth at La Grange, Georgia, on November 4; but the problem of maintaining "white supremacy"—a commanding desideratum of almost universal acceptance among white Southerners of Phillips' generation—still remained. Other remnants of the Old South persisted. Cotton culture and Negro labor dominated the agricultural scene as they had in ante-bellum years. New prophets were preaching diversification, whether in agricultural or industrial enterprise, but the fundamental concepts of Southerners yielded slowly to innovations. Adjustments had been made since 1865, and were still in the making; but habits of life and thought were not transilient. Accelerated industrialization was hardly as important as agrarian protests against "redeemer" governments.

Phillips' ancestry and early life remain nebulous themes despite a search for records and correspondence with contemporaries. He once wrote to Roland M. Harper, a classmate at the University of Georgia, that he was uninterested in genealogy, and Harper concluded that Phillips was "not proud of some of his ancestors." He did not mention his father, Alonzo Rabun Phillips, in his letters; but he often wrote affectionately of his mother, nee Jessie Elizabeth Young, who taught in a girls' school in Milledgeville and directed dressmaking and needlework in the Industrial College at Greensboro, North Carolina. Poor health soon terminated the Greensboro appointment; she joined her son in Madison; and in 1906 he recorded her death. Only twenty years his senior, she had been a "boon companion." Several of Phillips' maternal ancestors, including his mother, died comparatively young, which may explain some of his own physical weaknesses. He improved his health considerably as a student at Athens; daily laps around the Lumpkin Street reservoir conditioned him to set a new college record for the mile race in the spring of his senior year.

Choice bits of autobiography were recorded with literary artistry in *Life and Labor in the Old South*. "In happy childhood I played hide-and-seek among the cotton bales with sable companions; I heard the serenade of the katy-dids while tossing on a hot pillow, somewhat reconciled to the night's heat because it was fine for the cotton crop. . . . Later I followed the pointers and setters for quail in the broom-sedge, the curs for 'possums and 'coons in the woods, and the hounds on the trail of the fox." At the home of a great-uncle, with whom he visited in vacation time, "the backyard, shaded and sandy, was vocal with the joys and sorrows of white and black children." When eyestrain interrupted his college career, he planted, plowed, and chopped a crop of cotton, "gaining more in muscle and experience than in cash." As a boy he "had picked cotton for short periods as a diversion. But the harvest of this crop of my own brought pain of mind and body. My hands, cramped from the plow-stock, made no speed in snatching the fluffy stuff, and my six-foot stature imposed a stooping intolerable in its day-long continuance." By this time a desire for practical experience was appeased, a Negro woman and her children were employed to complete the task, and Phillips returned to college convinced "that none of the work was beyond the strength of a stripling, and the sunshine, though very hot, was never prostrating."

Other "recollections from a barefoot age" yield observations on rural life in upland Georgia. Phillips occasionally attended camp meetings at Warm Springs and Flat Rock in Meriwether and Heard counties, but his own county of Troup had outgrown primitive assemblages. At home the family attended Asbury Chapel on circuit-rider Sundays and enjoyed "a specially copious dinner" prepared "against the 'coming by' of a crowd of guests." Perhaps he participated in the annual "all day singing with dinner on the ground" as Methodists assembled to clear weeds and underbrush from graveyard and grove. "These customs had held on from preceding generations, along with the murmur of 'studying aloud' in the schoolhouse, whose session still avoided the months in which the children were needed to pick cotton."

To supplement local schools young Phillips attended the Tulane preparatory department in New Orleans. Then followed seven years at the University of Georgia, as undergraduate, graduate student, fellow, tutor, and assistant librarian, before he transferred at the turn of the century to study for the doctorate at Columbia University. His record at Tulane High School, where he graduated in 1893, and at the University of Georgia, where he received the bachelor of arts degree four years later, did not reveal unusual aptitude for history or foretell a career as a scholar. High-school marks were on the whole superior, with highest attainment in Greek; but an examination grade of 73 in junior history discouraged enrollment for another year in that subject. Performance as a freshman at Georgia reversed the ratings, for a grade of 93 in history and a perfect score in botany compensated for low marks in Latin and Greek, algebra and geometry, and English composition. His senior average of 93 indicated considerable improvement. A poor student of Latin until his fourth year, he did superior work in three years of French and two of mental science, and he also performed creditably in the biological and physical sciences. He made the honor roll in several classes, including history, although he never rated higher than sixth in his class in that subject.

The history offerings of Franklin College, the liberal arts division of the University of Georgia, were quite standard for that period. Under the direction of John H. T. McPherson, doctoral graduate of Johns Hopkins, the department prescribed general history and historical geography, political and constitutional history of England, United States history, and political economy with a presentist emphasis and an application of principles to American economic history. Phillips' ambition and McPherson's encouragement led the student to continue as a candidate for the master's degree, with courses in French and German, English constitutional history, readings in history and historiography, and federal and state constitutions. As a tutor in history, 1898–1900, Phillips taught a freshman class in general history and also the sophomore course in English history. According to McPherson, "He acquitted himself most creditably. His presence and manner in the class-room are good; he was at all times diligent, progressive, willing, cheerful, and self-controlled under the trials that often beset a young teacher." During Phillips' last year at Georgia, he served as assistant librarian as well as tutor; his interest in library work was sufficient to stimulate a desire to seek appointment as librarian after he acquired the doctorate, a post to which the chancellor was willing to appoint him.

In the midst of his work for the master's degree, Phillips attended the 1898 summer session at the University of Chicago, a fateful event in his career, for Frederick Jackson Turner was temporarily a member of the faculty. The

Georgia student enrolled in courses with Benjamin S. Terry and Ferdinand Schevill as well as in Turner's seminar on American colonial institutions. He also had opportunity to attend Turner's lectures on the history of the West. Phillips had already begun a study of ante-bellum Georgia politics as a master's thesis, later expanded into a dissertation at Columbia University and published as *Georgia and State Rights*. In its preface he wrote that "a very suggestive lecture by Dr. F. J. Turner upon American sectionalism" set him "to work some years ago to study the effect of nullification upon Georgia politics." A critique of Phillips contributed to *The Marcus W. Jernegan Essays in American Historiography* says that "Dunning's primary concern with political and constitutional problems" at Columbia "failed to arouse any responsive enthusiasm in his pupil." Rather, incentive was provided by the Turner lecture on American sectionalism which was Phillips' "light on the road to Damascus. It furnished him with the key to the subject with which he had been struggling in his dissertation." As the incentive had been provided "some years" before, the conclusion that the doctoral candidate, in the midst of his dissertation, found Dunning unsatisfying must be discarded. Despite Turner's stimulating lecture in 1898, Phillips went to Columbia to work with Dunning rather than to Wisconsin to study with Turner.

During his two years of residence at Columbia, Phillips worked with eminent scholars in history, economics, and international law. In American history he studied the colonies in the seventeenth and eighteenth centuries with Herbert Levi Osgood, from whom "he derived almost nothing"; political and constitutional history of the United States with John W. Burgess, who failed to impress Phillips favorably; and American political philosophy and the United States during the Civil War and Reconstruction with Dunning. He took several courses in the European field with James Harvey Robinson and William M. Sloane. In other departments Phillips studied the history of political economy and railroad problems with Edwin R. A. Seligman and diplomatic history with John Bassett Moore.

II

Phillips' formal education was completed in 1902, but he did not cease to be a learner when he left Columbia for a summer's tour of Europe and an instructorship in history at the University of Wisconsin. Turner's influence on his young colleague in the years from 1902 to 1908 manifested itself particularly in Phillips' two-volume *Plantation and Frontier* and here and there in other books and articles. Another master teacher, J. Franklin Jameson, contributed no less than Turner to the development of the ultimate scholar. That Phillips eventually became a precisionist in thought and phrase may be attributed in large measure to the editor of the *American Historical Review*. Seldom are editors of scholarly periodicals classified as teachers; yet Phillips and scores of other young historians discovered that they were in effect taking another seminar as they revised their manuscripts for publication in the review. Jameson's editorial correspondence is replete with wholesome suggestions for supplementary research, reorganization of material, compressing of evidence, and improvement of craftsmanship.

Some kindly and constructive criticism from the review's editor provided the spark that fired Phillips with enthusiasm to master the art of expression. After commending the young historian in 1905 for the mass of pertinent data he had assembled, Jameson chided him for careless presentation. Hastily constructed sentences revealed careless thinking. "You promise to do such excellent things in the way of historical investigation that I should heartily wish that you might take much more pains with your style." Phillips revised the paper and resubmitted it. "Thanks to your criticism," the author wrote, "it is, I am sure, materially improved. I hope you will keep it in mind that your criticism is the most valuable that I am able to get; please let me have bits of it in the future, on either style or substance." And then he added a fateful sentence that brought the criticism he invited, for Phillips wrote that he would soon submit two or three more papers to the review. He had not yet learned the lesson that quality rather than quantity is the proper measure of scholarship.

"I am glad to know that you are likely to have other articles for us," Jameson replied. "As to advice . . . you have a good deal of time before you and need be in no haste to publish. Secure reputations, valuable when a man is fifty or sixty, are not to be had but by taking a good deal of pains and time for the execution of everything that a man prints over his name while he is young." Jameson's word "pains," used in both letters, did not fall upon barren ground. It was not unusual for Phillips in later years to redraft articles and chapters a dozen times to achieve symmetry, rhythm, and balance. His repeated admonition, "The writer must take pains to save the reader pains," made a lasting impression upon students who sought precision in craftsmanship.

As a teacher Phillips excelled in seminar direction. He encouraged graduate students to investigate topics of their own choosing, even though they were far afield from his own major interest. But the student who thought his report might escape the critical eye of the master soon discovered that Phillips was acquainted with the sources. The director taught historical method by criticism of error rather than by prior instruction. If an early draft of a report or thesis were submitted with faulty method or fuzzy style, the patient professor would compress phrases into words, paragraphs into sentences, and painstakingly indicate gaps in research, defects in conclusion. If succeeding chapters revealed little improvement, they were returned with the advice that the writer must assume the major responsibility. Students might flounder, and many of them fell by the wayside, but those who profited from his counsel learned research and writing.

In his early years as a teacher Phillips performed his classroom duties enthusiastically, but after he attained recognition as a scholar, lecturing was a product of reluctant effort. His Old South course drew many students, some of whom enrolled for easy credit rather than a burning desire for knowledge. Class attendance was more or less optional; it dwindled until an examination was announced, and then for a week the classroom would be heavily populated and students would scurry to the reserve shelves to scan the contents of three or four books, for one of the questions was sure to involve collateral "reading." The examination over, with few grades less than the "Gentleman's C," attendance would again decline until another emergency brought a temporary revival of "study."

That Phillips gave little thought to preparation was apparent. The purpose of teaching, he said many times, was not to impart knowledge. He usually brought to class a hundred or so three-by-five cards from his files, and from these he might read for the whole period, sometimes with an interspersal of comment. Occasionally he would lay his notes aside and just talk about the South. If a new collection of correspondence yielded a lovers' tale, the cards from which he read provided "moonlight and magnolia" charm, and hence the undivided interest of the class. And if the instructor sang southern ballads and Negro spirituals, the absent members regretted their dereliction. Near the end of a semester he might announce that he planned to "take to the woods early," and students understood that the "woods" might mean his study where a book was in progress or the Southland where garrets yielded plantation records. If the announcement came a week before the Christmas holidays, and early departure meant a sojourn in the South, he might contrast its warm, sunny climate with rugged weather in the heart of Michigan—"if Michigan has a heart."

Despite unorthodox classroom procedure and unsystematic treatment of subject matter, students came to understand and appreciate the South no less than the genial, ruddy-faced teacher who seemed to personify both the culture and the tradition of his native region. They could forgive his neglect, for neglect was translated into the assembling of records and the publication of history. There was no diminution of respect or esteem.

Former students who recorded impressions of Phillips should be permitted to speak for themselves. A Detroit Negro attorney who attended two of Phillips' courses in southern history at Wisconsin and subsequently received a law degree from the University of Michigan recalled with pleasure not only the benefit from instruction but also the Southerner's "many courtesies . . . at the University and at the Maple Bluff Golf Club." A summer school student whose letter gives no indication of time and place remembered a "most enjoyable" experience and thanked him for "generosity in dramatizing and humanizing" the subject. Eighty-two students who enrolled in Phillips' courses at the University of Southern California during the summer of 1922 collectively expressed esteem "for the treasures in subject matter, the grasp of the purpose in studying history and the inspiration that your presence has been to us."

One of Phillips' doctoral students, Albert R. Newsome, appreciated his mentor's "grasp and interpretation of history" which "completely satisfied" his "desire to understand the real causes and effects of movements and events."

According to Chauncey S. Boucher, a member of the Michigan seminar saw a reference to the prospectus of *The Self-Instructor,* and inquired whether the proposed Charleston magazine had materialized. Phillips "offered to bet a dollar to a dough-nut, and later increased the odds to a dollar to a hole in the dough-nut, that the paper or magazine was never published." Several months later, Boucher, then in Charleston assembling material for his dissertation, discovered evidence that the first number had been issued. The records are silent as to whether Phillips paid the wager; as a devotee of poker he doubtless maintained his honor among gamblers in the classroom.

Hardly three and a half academic years remained to Phillips when he transferred to Yale University in the fall of 1930, but in that brief time he established himself firmly in the affections of his students. An undergraduate, Mac Parsons, who "refused to let all work and no play . . . make Mac a dull boy," remembered his "association" with Phillips as he read for honors in American history. His instructor's "understanding and complete command of subject surely made . . . [him] more sympathetic to learning than a thousand books could have done." His college education did not consist of "great knowledge" or "much wisdom, but a broad base of intellectual tolerance, background, and curiosity," and his course with Phillips was "the largest sortie into the citadel."

Eventually Phillips confined his teaching to southern history, but the neophyte at Wisconsin taught European and English history as well as the Old South. At Tulane University he supplemented his course in the Old South with graduate seminars on the nullification issue, Reconstruction, the slavery issue in federal politics, and the plantation system. Phillips' program at Michigan consisted of a sophomore survey class, an alternation of southern and western history, and a graduate seminar. One of the factors that induced him to accept an offer from Yale University in 1929 was a light teaching load and consequently more time for research and writing. His program there was limited to two courses, each of which met once a week for two hours: an undergraduate conference for honor students, with a maximum enrollment of fourteen, and a graduate seminar in American history.

III

Phillips' productive record was impressive, whether in quantity or quality. A zealous promoter of agricultural reform in the early years of the twentieth century, he published a score of pieces in Georgia newspapers; but the role of advocate, in which he exhibited considerable talent, seemed less inviting than the lure of scholarship. He wrote six volumes and edited four others; contributed more than fifty articles to professional journals, association reports, collaborative works, dictionaries, and encyclopedias; and reviewed forty-seven books. The pages Phillips wrote and edited during a period of little more than three decades serve as a monument to his industry.

Southern politics as a field of research appealed to Phillips at the threshold of his career as a productive scholar. His dissertation, *Georgia and State Rights,* an ante-bellum political subject with emphasis on federal relations, won the Justin Winsor prize in American history. He returned to a political theme to edit *The Correspondence of Robert Toombs, Alexander H. Stephens, and Howell Cobb,* an assemblage of documents which provided much of the evidence incorporated in the *Life of Robert Toombs.* Eventually he began a study of the Old South's public policy as a companion volume to *Life and Labor;* the fragment appeared posthumously as *The Course of the South to Secession.* A few of Phillips' contributions to *The South in the Building of the Nation* were political in nature, but his most significant articles in this area were "The South Carolina Federalists" and "The Southern Whigs," published respectively in the *American Historical Review* and *Essays in American History Dedicated to Frederick Jackson Turner*. Sketches of John C. Calhoun, William H. Crawford, Robert Y. Hayne, Alexander H. Stephens, and Robert Toombs appeared in the *Dictionary of American Biography;* of Jefferson Davis, Stephen A. Douglas, and Toombs in the *Encyclopaedia of the Social Sciences*. Phillips lamented to Allen Johnson that he had no talent for political biography, but the editor of the *Dictionary of American Biography* justifiably commended the sketch of Calhoun in warmest terms. Indeed, his brief biographies of southern statesmen were gems of perfection.

In his Wisconsin period Phillips assembled considerable material on Crawford with biographical intent, but paucity of private papers prompted abandonment of the project. Perhaps kind fate intervened; the historian's method of treatment and style of writing did not lend themselves easily to character delineation. That he lacked skill in comprehensive portraiture is indicated by the biography of Toombs. Phillips saw him as a product and a type rather than an individual, and he sought to use the Georgian's life as a focal point in presenting state and regional problems and policies. The biographer concluded "that Toombs was primarily an *American* statesman with nationwide interests and a remarkable talent for public finance, but the stress of the sectional quarrel drove him, as it had driven Calhoun before him, into a distinctly *Southern* partisanship at the sacrifice of his *American* opportunity." Turner and Justin H. Smith penned laudatory comments; the Harvard professor, who had watched his former colleague attain "a higher level each time" he wrote, commended him for making "a real person" of Toombs; and

Smith, who violated a lifelong rule by reading several chapters on the train, thanked him for revealing the man as well as the debater and legislator. Actually, Phillips did not succeed in making Toombs live again, for the Georgian was relegated to a "shadowy background" by political detail, the book's major contribution. The biography lacked "portraiture," said Nathaniel W. Stephenson; it neglected Toombs' personality, asserted William K. Boyd.

Despite genuine interest and modest achievement in political history, Phillips concluded that he could not understand that thread until he examined the South's social and economic structure. As a postdissertation subject he investigated the problem of transportation in ante-bellum South Carolina and Georgia. Before completing this task he began a compilation of documents illustrating southern plantation and frontier agricultural units. He then concentrated for several years on a study of Negro slavery in America. A compilation of Florida plantation records intervened before publication of his best known work, *Life and Labor in the Old South*. The subject matter of some of his books appeared first as articles; a few of his short monographs were unrelated to future volumes.

The dedication of *Transportation in the Eastern Cotton Belt*, "TO THE DOMINANT CLASS OF THE SOUTH," provides insight into Phillips' conception of southern history. In his thinking, that class included in a very special sense those southern whites whose economic power and political prestige gave ascendancy in life and labor. After the book was in proof the Columbia University Press Committee on Publication found an objectionable clause—"The Hell that is Called Reconstruction"—in the eulogy that followed the dedication. A true statement, the committee's secretary wrote the author, but its "appeal to sectional feeling" would be prejudicial to the university and its press. Phillips deleted the offensive words and sub-

stituted therefor "Troublous Upheaval and Readjustment."
The study is hardly a bypath; broadly conceived and exhaustively executed, it is an integral part of a plan for presenting the Old South in all of its ramifications. An intro-
ductory chapter surveys transportation in the whole
southern area. Throughout the volume, and particularly
in the chapters on the lowlands before 1800 and the up-
lands before the railroad era, Phillips articulated transportation with physiography, soil, population, climate,
crops, markets, prices, labor supply, planters, the plantation system, yeoman farmers, and merchants. Most internal-
improvement studies carry dullness to an extreme; Phillips'
volume escapes humdrum banality.

Soon after Phillips joined the Wisconsin staff, Richard
T. Ely inaugurated the American Bureau of Industrial
Research, which embarked upon a co-operative enterprise,
A Documentary History of American Industrial Society.
Separate publication of Phillips' *Plantation and Frontier*
volumes would have been a wise expedient, for they had
little vital connection with others in the series, the frontier
was northern as well as southern, and large agricultural
units in other sections of the country were unrepresented
in a study of slave-labor plantations. Phillips was chiefly
concerned with the production of "material goods" by organized society and with the effect of such "work and work-
grouping upon life, upon philosophy, and upon the internal and external relations of the society." In great areas
of the South "either the plantation system or the frontier
shaped the general order of life without serious rival,"
hence an examination of the two systems approximated "a
study of Southern industrial organization and society."
The effective influence of the two types cannot be denied,
but the editor's labored explanation of the work's design
cannot justify omission of the farm. The research of Frank
L. Owsley and his associates indicates a significance of that

agricultural unit, at least in the late ante-bellum period, that the editor did not sense.

In collaboration with James D. Glunt, Phillips had another opportunity to present raw materials of southern history in *Florida Plantation Records*. A fifty-page introduction by the senior editor is a masterly essay on plantation records in general and the records of two Middle Florida plantations in particular. Sundry inventories of human and physical property have value, but plantation journals and the overseers' reports to the absentee owner, reproduced in the crude and picturesque language and spelling of semiliterate men, are the most significant portions of the records. These important plantation functionaries were totally unaware that their correspondence and journals would be used by historians to reconstruct the life of which they were a part, and one does not therefore have to evaluate their records in terms of subtle meanings or questionable motivations.

It is doubtful if Phillips contemplated a more comprehensive treatment of ante-bellum economic and social life than that which appeared in *Life and Labor in the Old South*. The $2,500 prize offered by Little, Brown and Company for the best unpublished work in American history, an incentive which sped Phillips' pen, did not limit the scope of the work. In a sense, *Life and Labor* was a popularization of *American Negro Slavery*, but with sufficient change in subject matter to justify a new publication. The book had many commendable qualities; it also had some disappointing features. Every page bore eloquent testimony of the author's fullness of knowledge, ripe experience, and majestic poise. Apt quotation, a sense of humor, and artistic flavor lent literary charm to scholarly work. But the volume was weighted with plantations and their economy to the neglect of the plain people who received meager treatment in a brief chapter and parts of a few others. Mines and mills and factories, bankers and factors and merchants were neglected, and so were railroad builders, educational leaders, and the other professional classes. Emphasis upon agricultural industry was justifiable, but the picture was woefully incomplete as a result of concentration upon the upper brackets in southern society. As in earlier works, Phillips endeavored to present slavery and the Negro sympathetically, but southernism compromised his good intentions. He surveyed the southern scene from the hospitable atmosphere of the "big house"; a patrician who saw only fringes of friction on a tranquil tradition.

Evidence, conclusions, and method were so inextricable in Phillips' writings that the reader cannot appreciate the relation of data to consequence without comprehending procedure. He presented particulars; he seldom painted composites. Planters and plantations, overseers and slaves were specifically identified and individually considered. Meager amalgam prevented systematic recital, albeit a parade of particulars in logical sequence stimulated a sense of solidarity and completeness. The more he wrote, Phillips often said, the more reluctant he was to draw conclusions. Whether he realized it or not, interpretation was accomplished through an intelligible presentation of evidence which could not fail to elicit latent meaning. Purpose was satisfied if he recorded his conception of prevailing patterns and instances of exceptions to them.

Phillips regarded history as a humanity and a social study, never as a social science. Whenever he used the expression "scientific history," he had in mind a means to an end, not the end itself. A course in statistics at the University of Chicago did not convert him to systematic compilation of instances. He used statistics, particularly in his early writings, but as the stylist evolved from the monographer, they became less significant to his purpose. History as humanity had little space for such data; the few he used were woven unobtrusively into his text. He spoke of "the dull statistics crowding some of the chapters" of Howard W. Odum's *An American Epoch;* of the pages in Charles S. Johnson's *The Negro in American Civilization* which were "crowded and beclouded with statistics and summaries of answers to trivial questionnaires."

IV

A few historians used plantation records sparingly before Phillips became their chief consultant; he was the first scholar to make them a major source of information. New Orleans residence gave access to the tens of thousands of slave bills of sale in the notarial records office, to ship manifests in the customhouse, and to agricultural records in the lower Mississippi Valley. Whether at Madison, Ann Arbor, or New Haven—where he spent nine-tenths of his postdoctoral years—Phillips made frequent foraging expeditions into the South to press his quest for plantation diaries, journals, account books, correspondence, rare imprints, and a medley of miscellany.

Historians who have sought some hidden key to Phillips' interest in planters and plantations are unaware of a basic principle which motivated his own research and served as admonition to neophytes: the scholar should exploit whatever sources are readily available. He did not ignore the problem motive—a more accurate portrayal of the South—but it is highly probable that the existence of documentary collections was as important in suggesting the problem as in providing the answer. The accessibility of great collections of plantation records, a few in public depositories but most of them still in private possession, incited a thrill of discovery and a sense of preservation as well as a desire for exploitation.

Zest as a researcher did not wane as Phillips accumulated thousands of note cards and acquired stature as a
historian. His personal letters attest the eagerness with
which he sought new evidence and solicited lecture engagements to defray the cost of travel. They yield copious evidence of cordial reception by southern families who opened
their cellars of wines and garrets of manuscripts, or put him
on the trail of other planters' descendants who gave access
to historic treasures. To Wymberley Jones DeRenne's "two
tables," Phillips wrote in reviewing his benefactor's published catalogue of holdings, "the one enriched from an
ancestral cellar of sherries and madeiras, the other laden
at command with manuscripts and rare pamphlets, he
welcomed friends and students, as I can warmly testify."
Supplementing a quarter century of research, he devoted
the greater part of another year to examining records in
most of the southern states before penning *Life and Labor
in the Old South.*

A study of Phillips' personal and professional career
leads inevitably to the conclusion that he knew much of
the human and physical geography of the South firsthand.
Like Francis Parkman he sought the open road that led
to human understanding as well as to physical remains;
unlike Parkman, Phillips was "born and bred in the briar
patch," a nativity with some handicaps as well as many
advantages. A traveling companion on a month's tour of
Virginia from Tidewater to Valley witnessed Phillips' enthusiastic participation in community life to acquire authentic knowledge of southern thought and culture. He
"was no cloistered scholar," a Canadian historian observed.
"He lived and moved among men and knew that from the
humblest and most illiterate there might come some illumi-
nation of the life of the past which he was seeking to interpret." Educational service to Negro troops at Camp
Gordon during World War I and a sojourn in Africa as an

Albert Kahn traveling fellow in 1929–30 provided other "human documents, as important for a true understanding of his subject as the most authentic letters and diaries and account books."

While a knowledge of the human geography of Phillips' South was an asset in recapturing the atmosphere of the past, the written record was a more tangible indication of its life and labor. Phillips recognized the superiority of unconscious evidence; hence his esteem for contemporary writings that were not intended for the public eye. In selecting *Plantation and Frontier* documents, three qualities were determinative: "rareness, unconsciousness, and faithful illustration." An unpublicized participant would adhere more exactly "to facts and conditions" than a witness who wrote for posterity. Phillips returned to this theme in *American Negro Slavery*. Statutes "describe a hypothetical régime, not an actual one"; court records seldom penetrated to "questions of human adjustment" and "decisions were . . . largely controlled by the statutes." But "the letters, journals and miscellaneous records of private persons dwelling in the régime and by their practices molding it more powerfully than legislatures and courts combined" provided "intimate knowledge."

Unlike plantation records, unconscious in motive and continuous in design, travel accounts were defective in that they recorded "jottings of strangers likely to be most impressed by the unfamiliar, and unable to distinguish what was common in the régime from what was unique in some special case." Travelogues and other writings for the press embodied propaganda, yet Phillips used such "indispensable" sources to good effect. He classified Frederick Law Olmsted and William H. Russell as "expert observers." As to Olmsted, Phillips quoted, paraphrased, and cited him two dozen times in *American Negro Slavery*, less often in *Life and Labor in the Old South*. With few exceptions, Phillips used the traveler's books approvingly, although his dissent was considerably more pronounced than his selections would indicate. The historian knew the South more accurately and more thoroughly than Olmsted; hence he rejected many statements in his travel accounts. One censor's observation that the southern historian distrusted the traveler because of a supposed "uncontrollable animus against the South" should be balanced against Phillips' classification of Olmsted as an "expert." The critical observation, "I believe that a fuller and more accurate knowledge of the late antebellum South can be obtained from the volumes of Olmsted than from Professor Phillips' own writings," has sensational appeal, but it demonstrates shallow knowledge of Olmsted, Phillips, and the South.

We have seen that a crusading spirit prompted Phillips to write southern history because he believed it had been neglected and distorted in nineteenth-century works. As northern historians had a near monopoly upon historical productivity, the standard histories set a pattern which would endure until less prejudiced accounts corrected it. One-sided presentation of controversial issues was not solely attributable to absence of objectivity, however, for a dearth of primary sources at institutions where history was written, Phillips said, resulted in substitution of "conjecture for understanding," as in Henry Adams' inadequate treatment of southern Federalists. Except for "mere surface politics," Phillips thought, the Old South was "largely an unknown country to American historians."

In common with other young southern historians, Phillips readily admitted that the South must share the responsibility for the inadequacy of its recorded history. There were apologias aplenty from the pens of partisans, but the South had done little during the last third of the nineteenth century to provide correct information on the

Old South or the new. A correct picture could not be presented, Phillips believed, until Southerners, trained in scientific method, delved into the records and made the truth available to anyone who sought a dispassionate concept of the South's positive role as one of the nation's sections. Eventually historians from other regions and countries might criticize, supplement, and correct the writings of native Southerners, but for the present "the great need seems to be that of interpretation of developments in the South by men who have inherited southern traditions."

This conviction—that southern history should be written by Southerners—was not peculiar to Phillips as he surveyed the problem at the opening of the twentieth century. It was shared by Dodd and Fleming and, indeed, by most historians of the South who began their labors in the first quarter of this century. They were wrong, of course; and they were also right. Historians who "inherited southern traditions" could advance revision but they could hardly attain an ultimate. American history in 1900 was unbalanced: the West as well as the South was still subordinated to the East. Both "sections" found spokesmen before the turn of the century, however, for Turner at Wisconsin and Dunning at Columbia were already changing the course of historiography. Virginia-born Woodrow Wilson and other Southerners trained in the Adams seminar at Hopkins were laboring to the same end. A beginning had been made, but only a beginning.

The problem of the South was greater than that of the West, for eleven southern states had played truant in the sixties and many Southerners in the border states had defied authority in that decade. More than that, white Southerners had held Negroes in bondage in an age of enlightenment, and some of them had defended the practice. The Civil War had settled that issue, but Southerners persisted in their nonconformity: their race problem seemed so insuperable that they continued the white-supremacy rationale beyond the point of contrary proof. Westerners were Americans—more Americanized than Easterners, Turner thought. Sons of the South were different. An Ohio River ferryman said so whenever he approached the northern bank: "We are nearing the American shore."

A critical appraisal of Phillips' writings should be predicated upon an awareness of the historian's own concept of his task as well as upon imperfections in attaining it. Acknowledging an appreciative letter which voiced a single criticism of *Life and Labor*—that modesty prevented the author from expressing his own views—Phillips replied that even the lament was pleasant, "for it says what I want my readers to gather—that I am not an authority primed with opinions but a student seeking to attain and to spread understanding." Many years earlier he put the matter strikingly in discussing slave codes of ante-bellum years. The "frankly repressive" regulatory laws "permit no apology," he asserted, "yet they invite explanation, for they were enacted and reënacted by normal representatives of normal American citizens, commonplace, acquisitive, fearful of disorder, resentful of outside criticism, and prone to cherish accustomed adjustments even if they put to scorn their own eloquence on each Fourth of July." If outsiders doubted that Southerners were "normal American citizens," he would remind them that slavery was not always a "peculiar" southern institution: that in the eighteenth century, certainly an age of enlightenment, it was of hemispheric legality; that it existed in all the eastern commonwealths from Maine to Pennsylvania; that moral scruples did not in the early period prevent ancestors of abolitionists from holding human beings in bondage. His interest in slavery therefore transcended the limits of the South with the view of putting the institution in proper perspective.

To accomplish his purpose, Phillips directed attention to the existence of slavery in the North, to the presence of a race problem wherever Negroes lived, to the relative ease with which northern states could solve the simple social and economic problem attending the emancipation of a few slaves, and to the insuperable parallel problem of effecting that desideratum wherever Negroes were a strong minority or an actual majority of the population. He admitted the evils of slavery and balanced the contributions of the institution to the advancement of the Negro with illustrations of protests against the enforced regime and admissions of slavery's shortcomings as a civilizing factor. In his early writings irritation occasionally came to the surface; as Phillips developed into a quiet patrician he acquired the ability to submerge annoyance beneath a tolerant understanding of sectional variation.

Speaking of New Englanders in general, he observed normal attitudes in the colonial period: "Shrewd in consequence of their poverty, self-righteous in consequence of their religion, they took their slave-trading and their slave-holding as part of their day's work and as part of God's goodness to His elect." While Massachusetts laws "were enforced with special severity against the blacks" in the late ante-bellum period, the colony's policy "merits neither praise nor censure; it was merely commonplace." Climate, economy, and poverty kept Negro slavery "negligible" in Plymouth and New Haven, Maine and New Hampshire. In New Jersey, where the code approximated New York's, the leader of an "alleged conspiracy" received capital punishment; "his supposed colleagues [lost] their ears only." Slaves guilty of ordinary crimes were often sentenced "to burning at the stake," with neighbors turning "honest shillings by providing faggots for the fire." An abundance of advertisements for absconding slaves in Pennsylvania newspapers indicated severity, but this impression was partly nullified by travelers' accounts which stressed a kindly regime. "The spirit not of love but of justice and the public advantage" terminated bondage in northern commonwealths.

V

With perspective established, Phillips narrowed his interest in slavery to the southern commonwealths and especially to Virginia and the Cotton Kingdom. His findings were unacceptable to some scholars who shared the field and to some critics who did not. Among the reproofs: He treated "slavery as a commercial enterprise rather than an evil"; he could not "fathom the negro mind"; he painted an aberrant picture of relations between master and slave; his neglect of such subjects as miscegenation illustrated "great powers of intellectual resistance"; he drew his data too exclusively from atypical large plantations; he devoted little attention to urban slaves; he tended "to argue to the contrary when facts seem to be unfavorable to the slaveholders."

Certain conclusions emerge with pellucid import from Phillips' writings. The institution of slavery was a civilizing factor; slaveholders were kindly and sympathetic masters; slaves were happy and contented laborers; the plantation system was an efficient method of transforming crude and inept brawn into productive enterprise; white Southerners insisted that the South was and should remain a white man's country. As categorical statements these findings are of course untenable, but all except the last were presented with qualifying limitations. Slavery as a civilizing factor "was restricted by the fact that even its aptest pupils had no diploma in prospect which would send them forth to fend for themselves"; cruel and malicious masters imposed their wills upon an inferior people; dissatisfied slaves demonstrated discontent through abscondings and revolts; planters failed as a result of discipline that was too lax or too stringent. The differences between Phillips and his censors resolve themselves into the problem of what was the rule and what the exception.

It would be difficult to prove that Phillips consciously suppressed evidence favorable to the Negro or unfavorable to the slaveholder in the documents he used. He seemed to be ever alert for instances of abscondings, revolts, miscegenation, or any other factors that illustrated maltreatment by whites or protests by blacks. But as he contemplated neither an orthodox synthesis nor a systematic presentation of every facet of slavery, he did not assemble in any one place all the examples of grievances that came to his attention, nor did he search all sources for evidences of them. Perhaps he thought that his illustrations were sufficient to indicate the presence of such evils. As an instance, limited space devoted to sexual relations between white men and slave women is not a measure of the historian's recognition of the abuse. A variety of data including census counts of mulattoes yielded explicit statements in several publications. Concubinage, he wrote in *Life and Labor,* "was flagrantly prevalent in the Creole section of Louisiana, and was at least sporadic from New England to Texas."

Absconding was a customary means of indicating discontent with slavery's restrictions; insurrection a more disconcerting method. Newspapers as well as most of the plantation records Phillips analyzed revealed instances of flight, and he seemed to be particularly interested in bringing them to his readers' attention. As "contentment must be mental as well as physical," adequate provision of vital necessities might not solve the problem. Running away meant temporary or permanent loss of property; revolt might well entail loss of life. Negro crimes of whatever sort, Phillips wrote, were viewed with considerable serenity if they involved only one individual, but "news or suspicion of concerted action . . . caused widespread alarm and uneasiness." Slave revolts were not only indicators of aggressive slave action against rigorous restraint but also tangible evidence of imperfect social and economic adjustment.

Critics have cited the docile attitude Phillips ascribed to Negroes and the limited number of group rebellions he discussed as indications of faulty understanding and inadequate research. Herbert Aptheker, whose *American Negro Slave Revolts* stresses "restlessness, discontent, and rebelliousness," asserted that Phillips presented limited data on revolts to maintain "racialistic notions that led him to describe the Negro as suffering from 'inherited ineptitude,' and as being stupid, negligent, docile, inconstant, dilatory and 'by racial quality submissive.' " Aptheker insisted "that discontent and rebelliousness were not only extremely common, but, indeed, characteristic of American Negro slaves."

Submissiveness and docility, like discontent and rebelliousness, are human rather than racial traits, possessed in varying degrees by members of any group. One has only to ponder the labor movement that began in the United States over a century ago to observe that white laborers tolerated long hours and poor pay while their employers grew rich in wealth and privilege; that farmers and laborers did not combine on a grand scale to overthrow monopoly; that economic protests did not reach revolutionary proportions despite sporadic strikes and other evidences of discontent. Negro slaves were too human to depart radically from customary behavior. Ignoring rumor, upon which Aptheker often depends, the tangible evidence of slave revolt is sufficient to indicate the human quality of protest, accentuated by a factor that made considerable difference: as Phillips expressed it, slaves "were deprived of the privileges and ambitions which commonly keep freemen self-restrained." This is hardly the language of a historian whose "racialistic notions"—which he undoubtedly possessed—

prompted exclusion of evidence. His conclusions were another matter.

Phillips' writings on slave revolts, as on many other aspects of slavery, did not exhaust all the evidence. Following customary procedure he demonstrated that they were
not peculiar to the South; "signal disturbances" in colonial
New York "were more notable for the frenzy of the public
than for the formidableness of the menace." Among an un-
certain number who plotted insurrection were slaves "too
doggedly barbaric to submit to industrial discipline" and
an increasing number "of high-grade, intelligent, self-
reliant negroes, mulattoes, and quadroons who were too
restless" under the system's restraints. As a result, anxiety
was greater and its effect in molding policy more significant,
Phillips concluded, than earlier historians realized. He
was as interested in the consequence of revolts and rumors
thereof as he was in what actually happened. Rebellions
and plots produced disquiet, and frequent rumors promoted "a fairly constant undertone of uneasiness." Under
such conditions advancement toward liberalism was considerably restrained.

Conspiracies and revolts brought reconsideration of
statutory regulations; new laws were enacted or old ones
revised "to make assurance increasingly sure that the South
should continue to be 'white man's country.'" Statutes,
however, provided an inaccurate picture of either the economic or the social regime, for except in times of stress and
strain they were laxly enforced, if enforced at all. Preroga-
tive rather than law, Phillips concluded, actually regulated
slaves. It followed logically in his thinking that "government of slaves was for the ninety and nine by men, and
only for the hundredth by laws." He characterized the
regime as "a paternalistic despotism," usually benevolent
but sometimes oppressive, "borne with light heartedness,
submission and affection by a large number of the blacks"

but "resented and resisted" by others. Ideal administration, Phillips thought, might "be symbolized by an iron hand in a velvet glove. Sometimes the velvet was lacking, but sometimes the iron. Failure was not far to seek in either case."

After studying the South and slavery for two decades, Phillips contrasted the extremes of the regime: "injustice, oppression, brutality and heartburning" on the one hand; "gentleness, kind-hearted friendship and mutual loyalty" on the other. In a mellow mood, stimulated by his own excursions into the past, he could write: "For him . . . who has known the considerate and cordial, courteous and charming men and women, white and black, which that picturesque life in its best phases produced, it is impossible to agree that its basis and its operation were wholly evil." "Some of the males of each race grew into ruffians, others into gentlemen in the literal sense, some of the females into viragoes, others into gentlewomen; but most of both races and sexes merely became plain, wholesome folk of a somewhat distinctive plantation type."

VI

In presenting a dynamic view of the plantation system, Phillips approached the Turner hypothesis closer than in any other part of his writing. Other historians and some economists held a static view of southern agricultural industry. Without regard for time or place, large, small, and nonslaveholders tilled their acres, many or few: the first with supervised slave labor; the second with a mixed group consisting of the owner, his family, and his slaves; the last with his own labor and that of his family. This was a still-life picture of southern industrial economy, a necessary "preface to the study of the dynamic forces" which shaped society and determined public policy.

Except for the element of slavery, the dynamic view conformed to the Turner pattern. Primitive industry, self-sufficient economy, and rudimentary society characterized the South's wilderness frontiers. The requirement of versatility declined and the importance of routine advanced as soon as the settler produced a surplus and established outside commercial ties. But at this point, when capital should have accumulated and systems of industry and society developed normally according to European and northern patterns, a planter invasion brought cheaper labor and a more effective routine. This "fixed routine," an application of the "factory system" to agricultural industry, was the only means "by which the unintelligent, involuntary negro labor could be employed to distinct advantage; and, other things being equal, the most successful planter was always he who arranged the most thorough and effective routine."

As new districts adapted to the plantation regime were opened to exploitation, the process of competition was repeated: the plantation encroached upon the farm and, with the rising cost of slave labor as the nineteenth century advanced, planters competed among themselves. Economy in purchasing supplies, marketing crops, and administering labor gave large holders an advantage and contributed to concentrated slaveholdings. "The final stage, reached in a few districts, was either a change to varied industry to which the plantation system was unsuited, or the partial depopulation of the country through the exodus of all the most energetic producers to new and more attractive lands." Superficial variations appeared, "but fundamentally the conditions and the development were a simple process, repeated in one area after another." Phillips attached great significance to this dynamic view, for "industry and society while apparently static were really in continuous motion and change. Affairs proceeded much in a routine; but no repetition of process was ever quite identical with its preceding occurrence. The routine itself was essentially dynamic. Impelled by the forces of competition and directed by the requirements of capitalized industry, the plantation régime promoted the growth of slaveholding accretions and extended the black belts wherever gang labor could be made the most effective system."

While the energies of the white people were hardly paralyzed because slavery stigmatized labor, the system nevertheless diminished productivity. It limited the opportunity of poor whites to earn wages, restricted the amount of capital available to the middle class and tempted members to invest earnings in slaves, and promoted leisure among an unusually large number of aristocrats. "The proportion of white collars to overalls and of muslin frocks to kitchen aprons was greater than in any other Anglo-Saxon community of equal income."

Phillips' overweening interest in the planter aristocracy and its human and physical property has already been indicated. His brief excursions into the history of nongentry classes indicate some knowledge of their contributions to the exploitation of southern resources. "It is regrettable," he wrote, "that data descriptive of small plantations and farms are very scant. Such documents as exist point unmistakably to informality of control and intimacy of white and black personnel on such units." He was quite aware of the numerical importance of small landholdings, but the lower classes did not excite his interest. Perhaps he was too content to permit paucity of readily accessible records to serve as an excuse for brevity in treating them. Had he exploited the manuscript census reports for 1850 and 1860 and the court records of sample counties, a plethora of data would have been at his command. A thousand courthouses from the Potomac to the Rio Grande yield evidence pertinent to their history, although even this largely unexploited source of information provides more data about the gentry than the plain people, for aristocrats had more property to bequeath, heir, or defend than their less opulent neighbors. Still, they yield tangible evidence on the social as well as the economic status of the plain people; and the manuscript census reports are a mine of information on these two aspects of all social classes.

VII

While Phillips confined most of his research and writing to the ante-bellum period, an occasional article of his early years dealt with problems of the New South; of his later years with the cause of secession and civil war. He made it abundantly clear in his lectures on the Old South that a paucity of statesmanlike leadership in the last ante-bellum decade led to the disastrous culmination of 1860–61, but his clearest published statement of causation appeared in a Memorial Day address delivered in 1931 at Yale University. Eloquent in phrase and succinct in thought, the speech of less than seven hundred words summarized the conclusions of a mature student of southern society. In his own Southland the commemoration came earlier, for April rather than May yielded flowers "in fullest bloom"; but the southern spirit was not essentially different from that which prevailed in the North: "a resolve in grief that the flower of American youth, a long lifetime ago, shall not have been killed or crippled in vain; that national peace, nobility, justice and wisdom shall be drawn from that carnage."

The cause of the carnage? "With every passing year of thoughtful research a belief grows wider and stronger that the war of the 'sixties was not an irrepressible conflict but a calamity of misguided zeal and blundering." Slaves in Kansas Territory, reduced to two on the eve of secession, sparked the crisis. In that vast area "two slaves were in plain purport the equivalent of none. But in the politics of the time they were the equivalent of two thousand or two million. In heated controversy they and the law concerning them had become a symbol, a portent, a touchstone."

Why did a nonexistent problem become a symbol of portentous magnitude? Southern-rights advocates sought a share of the national territory as a gesture that the North did not intend to overturn the South's scheme of life. Without the token, acquiescence "would bring a sequence of aggressions until an overpowering North would impose a fanatical will, carrying industrial paralysis and social chaos." Northern champions, "deeming these fears to be groundless and suspecting a conscious exaggeration, refused the token. Peacemakers, in a desperate effort which is now well-nigh forgotten, failed to find any formula for solution or postponement."

The result? "Secession came, and the denial of its validity; Fort Sumter and the choice of dread evils by the states of the Upper South; the panoply of war, the dust and mud and heat and cold and hunger and thirst of marching men, the fumes and roar of battle, the shock of bullet and shell, the groan and gasp of the dying, amputation in rough hospitals, misery beyond the telling in prison camps, anxiety and anguish of loved ones at home. There was invasion and grim devastation; and at long last Appomattox, as an end yet not an end."

Not an end because "war's objective is peace, but war's cult of hatred persists beyond the laying down of arms and sets the peace askew. The victor is prone to fix the terms at his own will and whim, to grind the face of the prostrate foe. 'Reconstruction ["The Hell that is Called Reconstruction" Phillips had said a quarter of a century before] is imposed; but an imposed reconstruction will not fit the case, for it is uninformed, ill-considered, and arbitrary. It must be painfully remodeled before a workable regime is attained again and a normal course of policy resumed. Thus if war chances to settle one problem it raises a host of others in its train." The conflict "came through default of state-craft, it imperilled the nation on doubtful occasion, and, to the general detriment, it diverted public notice then and for years afterward from genuine to false issues. The memories of its heroism are a pride; the thought of its cost is a sorrow."

The Memorial Day orator at Yale spoke a few weeks later at Blacksburg, Virginia, to descendants of Southerners "who stood apart from the carnage" of the sixties. Their "personal neutrality" in that repressible conflict deserved no "censure," for the war, he repeated, was "a fruit of excessive and misguided zeal by fervid partizans of the North and the South." But his auditors shared a responsibility with black-belt Southerners whose ancestors believed white supremacy was imperiled by "Africanization and ensavagement." The universal obligation was a preservation of "The Historic Civilization of the South"—a wholesome civilization despite its fallacies. "It has now changed, is changing, and will continue to change," Phillips asserted. "Yet in essentials it has persisted through fair times and foul, and will persist. Its tradition of kindliness, hospitality, honesty, moderation, and good humor is a precious possession, to be cherished and spread abroad." As a symbol of that historic civilization, he pointed to the "Faithful Servant" John whose family honored him in death as it loved him in life, and whose name was legion. The faithful John did not create a problem of race. "It is a characteristic of Southerners in the plantation tradition," Phillips wrote aphoristically, "that they disesteem Negroes in the mass while esteeming them individually, whereas the rest of the world is inclined to dislike them individually while tending to champion their cause in the mass."

After residing alternately in the South and the North, Phillips regarded himself as "a somewhat denatured Southerner"; actually he had lost little of his southernism. He was grateful when Negro students enrolled in his classes; twentieth-century Southerners should, in their own interest, emulate the example set by masters and mistresses of ante-bellum plantations—" 'catch them young and bring them up in the way they should go.'" He regretted the racial chasm that had developed. Intelligent Negroes of his generation had no desire to destroy civilization. But the great mass of Negroes, though "not without likeable and admirable traits," were not ready for "full fellowship of any sort in a democratic civilized order." They were unprepared to exercise the right to vote effectively and intelligently.

A descendant of the Old South was speaking, and much that he said was true; but it was not the whole truth. Phillips was spokesman for the dominant class of the South; a mellowed intellectual patrician who saw the Negro through the eyes of a kindly master, understood his weaknesses, and appreciated his faithfulness and loyalty; who stressed lack of talent rather than lack of opportunity as explanation of inferior status; and who minimized the Negro's quest for freedom and civil rights. He was essentially a historian of aristocracy, incidentally of slavery. His primary interest was the plantation system of which slaves were an integral part. But the system was organized and to some extent dominated by an economic and social aristocracy, and its historian was as handicapped in viewing the pyramid from its base as a captain of industry would be in writing a balanced history of the factory system. Phillips, like the business magnate, could fathom the laborer's mind as far as vocal expressions and surface reactions permitted but not to the depths of inner consciousness.

Historically speaking, Phillips' central theme of southern history was correct, for white Southerners from colonial days to the twentieth century advocated white supremacy. The theory was not peculiar to the South: the white race everywhere found it a convenient and acceptable explanation of progress and enlightenment on the one hand, of quiescence and illiteracy on the other. But before Phillips' generation closed, a new scholarship repudiated racial inferiority and found other accounting for the economic, social, and cultural backwardness of nonwhite people. Unfortunately for Phillips, all of his basic views were the product of his early research and thought; within a decade after he attained the doctorate his concepts were formulated. The next twenty years of research and writing lacked dynamic quality; they were devoted to ampliations and refinements of ideas already expressed. Despite imperfections and imbalance, the static view was a contribution, for it presented aspects of southern history theretofore unexploited and it relegated to limbo much that had passed for history of the South in the preceding generation.

CHAPTER FOUR

Walter Lynwood Fleming
Historian of Conservatism

"IT IS NECESSARY, I think, as well as important to have the younger generation of Southerners understand the actual conditions following the Civil War, but the trouble is that from anything in print they are likely to get either a false impression or at best an imperfect one. The other side has hitherto done all the writing talking and printing. The Southern people have not rushed into books with their knowledge of things. Consequently, the younger generation knows little of the post bellum troubles except thro' tradition, which is not very lasting, and thro' prejudiced accounts written in Mass. or Ohio."

Walter Lynwood Fleming wrote these words in 1903 as he assembled material for his Columbia University dissertation on *The Civil War and Reconstruction in Alabama*. The period he was investigating was no further removed from the turn of the century than the New Deal is from Americans of 1955. Yet the recent past of Fleming's day was infinitely more controversial than the yesterday of our own, and the sectional and cultural milieu of the sixties and seventies set history more askew than polemics of the 1930's. Retrospects of Reconstruction were no more satisfying to Fleming than chronicles of crises were to Phillips, and the Alabamian, like the Georgian, delved into contemporary records to correct the past and inform the future. He succeeded only in part: the conservative mold in which he reached maturity limited his achievement. Yet he made progress as he outgrew southern provincialism, and *The*

Sequel of Appomattox presented a fairer view of the dismal decade than the Alabama study.

I

Fleming's early life is the familiar story of an ambitious and talented farm boy inspired by great teachers to seek knowledge and use it effectively. Born on a plantation near Brundidge, Alabama, he heard stories of scalawags and carpetbaggers from his Confederate cavalryman father, William LeRoy Fleming, and thus early acquired an interest in the era into which he was born on April 7, 1874. Farm chores, rural schools, and the local academy provided normal development in formative years. What good fortune brought him to Alabama Polytechnic Institute in the early 1890's is a matter of conjecture, but matriculation at that agricultural and mechanical college juxtaposed an apt pupil and a master teacher, George Petrie, whose gift for inspiring students with a genuine love for history became traditionary.

Fleming's mentor at Auburn was only eight years his senior and still in his twenties when the student from southeastern Alabama entered the state's leading institution of higher learning. With bachelor's and master's degrees from the University of Virginia, where he studied with competent teachers, Petrie cast his lot with Johns Hopkins University as a candidate for the doctorate. He fully intended to take his degree in romance languages, but the stimulating teaching of Herbert Baxter Adams and Amelia B. Edwards, Egyptologist, changed his interest to history. Courses in economics with Richard T. Ely, in political science with George H. Emmott, in history with John M. Vincent, and series of lectures by Woodrow Wilson, J. Franklin Jameson, and James Schouler gave breadth and depth to his learning. Petrie returned to Auburn as professor of history and Latin, well equipped in subject matter, endued with an infectious enthusiasm for history, and indoctrinated with new concepts of education.

Petrie's philosophy and methodology of history are noteworthy, for they were a new departure at Auburn and a rarity anywhere in American education. "In this department," he wrote, "the aim is not so much to memorize facts as to understand them. . . . The students are taught to investigate the growth of ideas and institutions, the rise and progress of great historical movements, and the reciprocal influences of men and circumstances." The instructor would constantly endeavor "to stimulate . . . wider reading and research in the library." It was not uncommon in the closing years of the nineteenth century for departments of history to speak of "laboratory work" in the subject. Advanced courses might be designated as seminaries, but instructors pointed with pride to "laboratory" equipment in their classrooms: books and magazines, manuscripts and maps, charts and diagrams, and tables, cases, shelves, and walls utilized to display them. The word "seminar" had little to recommend it in an agricultural and mechanical college, and Petrie conducted courses for juniors, seniors, and graduates "by the laboratory method" to elevate the subject to the level of a science in a school that stressed technology. "Emphasis is laid," he said, "on the importance of securing proper material for investigation and every incentive is given to the collection and use of new documents, papers and letters illustrative of Southern, and especially of Alabama history."

These statements that Petrie put into the Polytechnic catalogue were not idle and meaningless words. Behind them was a dynamic and inspiring personality that gave them literality. Influence upon students who came under his tutelage cannot be measured, but Fleming and a dozen others continued the study of history in reputable graduate schools, and several of them attained recognition as historical scholars.

Measured in terms of courses in history, Fleming's training at Alabama Polytechnic Institute seems meager indeed. His work with Petrie, undergraduate and graduate, consisted of one year in English history and two in American. Apparently he had mastered the fundamentals of the subject before he entered college, for he passed examinations in the freshman and sophomore courses upon enrolling. Except for research papers, history students at Auburn devoted little time to highly specialized and narrow segments of knowledge, but the professor's constant insistence upon the use of original materials promoted independent thinking. Whatever the quantity or quality of training, Fleming attained the B.S. degree in 1896 and the M.S. degree a year later. From 1896 to 1900 he served variously as an instructor in English and history, as an assistant librarian, and as a second lieutenant and quartermaster during the Spanish-American War. These years were fruitful in expanding his knowledge through affluent reading. When, in 1900, he applied for admission to eastern graduate schools, he had read more than one hundred and fifty volumes of history and biography. Thirty-seven of them treated the South or southern leaders; the others represented a wide range of interests and many countries. His research in this period soon materialized in a paper entitled "The Buford Expedition to Kansas," which appeared in the *American Historical Review* and later in expanded form in the Alabama Historical Society *Transactions*.

If Fleming aspired to follow in Petrie's footsteps, it seemed natural that he should go to Johns Hopkins University for graduate work under Adams' direction. His application for a fellowship there was supported by Petrie's strong endorsement of "one of our crack men," by the Buford manuscript, and by the list of history books he had read. Perhaps it was fortunate that the fellowship did not materialize, for Adams was in poor health and died the next year. From 1900 forward, southern historical scholars were attracted to Columbia University, as they had been to Hopkins during the previous decade or so. As late as July, 1900, Fleming seemed committed to Harvard University, but in the fall of the year he entered Columbia to work with another great teacher, William A. Dunning, whose sympathetic treatment of the war and Reconstruction periods ingratiated him with a growing southern clientele.

The southern scholar who goes north to school has more difficulty in adjusting himself to the climate than to the people. Within a few months Fleming came to appreciate most of his new acquaintances at Columbia, but more than a year after transferring to New York City he wrote Thomas M. Owen: "If I ever live to get out of Yankeedom I'll nev[er] come back. The weather is so fearful." But the weather did not impede his quest for the doctorate. The roster of professors with whom he took courses is a roll call of some of the ablest scholars in America. He studied economics with Edwin R. A. Seligman, sociology with Frank R. Giddings, and political science with John Bassett Moore and John W. Burgess. In history he took work with Dunning, Herbert L. Osgood, William M. Sloane, and James Harvey Robinson. Study with these men gave the student a liberal education and clear perspective, albeit his dissertation, written under Dunning's direction, revealed the author's southern conservatism.

II

Louisiana State University was still an adolescent institution of higher learning when Fleming was appointed professor of history in 1907 after three productive years at West Virginia. An enrollment of five hundred students, a faculty of less than fifty members, and state and federal appropriations that barely exceeded $75,000 stood in sharp contrast with the creditable university that was born a quarter of a century later. Some important problems had been resolved a year or two before Fleming arrived: Tulane University was denied state support, colleges of agriculture and law were established, and, thanks to Thomas D. Boyd's farsightedness, the school became coeducational. But the university had not yet come of age, and the College of Arts and Sciences was still an ephemeral division. Complacency dominated the academic atmosphere. An ambitious scholar found little inspiration in a school that did not rise above mediocrity, and Fleming's correspondence resembles a book of lamentations.

"I am convinced that you are not as busy as I am," he wrote to Roulhac Hamilton after a month in Baton Rouge. "I have just moved, have 18 hours a week of work, 2 hrs being on Saturday, one class of dead heads the worst I ever had anywhere, two fine babies, 4 & 2 yrs—all these keep one busy." As early as 1911 he was seriously contemplating searching for a better position because of excessive work. A year later he admitted that history was thriving if "numbers and annual increase" served as criteria, but an enrollment of a hundred students in his freshman class, a teaching load of nineteen hours, and burdensome committee work left little time for research and writing. The library was poorly equipped in any field of history. A total of some six hundred books on the South, an annual allowance of $200 to spend for books in American history, a few broken files of Louisiana newspapers, with none for the period 1830–60, and an incipient pamphlet collection were other reasons why Fleming became dissatisfied. But the condition that irritated him most was the state's "craze of 'practical' education" which cheapened learning at high school and college levels and absorbed resources in agricultural and experiment station work and "demonstration trains." "Besides," he said, "we have too many cheap, unscholarly professors, a state of affairs which throws all progressive administrative work upon a few men, while the rest act as a drag."

Despite Fleming's complaints that teaching and committee responsibilities precluded scholarly activity, his publication record for the decade at Louisiana State University was far from mediocre. He assembled a mass of material on Jefferson Davis and wrote sundry articles on that southern leader, he continued research on the Ku Klux Klan, he published a volume on William Tecumseh Sherman as a college president, and he began a history of the university. But committee work became increasingly irksome, and when Vanderbilt University offered him the Holland N. McTyeire professorship of history in 1917, he accepted it. Ironically, he was soon more heavily involved in administrative work than before. In 1923 he became dean of the College of Arts and Sciences and a few years later director of graduate work. His able planning materialized in scholarly development and expansion through the aid of Rockefeller funds. A genuine desire for the quiet role of historian was an unrealized goal.

Few historians today appreciate the handicaps under which southern scholars labored forty or fifty years ago. No one understood better than Fleming the South's limitations and inadequacies that must be overcome before its historians could write with fullness and freedom. In 1912 he informed Professor Eugene C. Barker of the University of Texas that the Confederate Museum in New Orleans desired to deny use of its holdings to "all who would not make firm promises to write 'sound' history, a promise which, of course, any decent scholar could not make, no matter how 'sound' his views may be." This attitude was being liberalized, he thought, but he knew of other "authorities" who would not permit use of their records unless research scholars would "accept absolutely their point of view." By way of contrast he pointed to the departments of archives and history in Alabama, Mississippi, and West Virginia, where research materials were accessible to all scholars.

In reply to Barker's question addressed to several southern historians, "What, in your opinion, is the cure for histories unfair to the South?" some answered that more history written by scientifically trained Southerners would contribute to that end, others that "time" alone would effect a remedy. A few opinions transcended provincialism. Roulhac Hamilton advised "less unreasonable denunciation of Northern writers." He had no sympathy with Southerners who insisted that if a book did not emulate Fightin' Joe Wheeler's order to American troops during the Spanish-American War—"Give the Yanks h——l!"—it was unfair to the South.

Fleming explained his views frankly. Southerners should write more history, and thus provide northern historians with correct data for their syntheses. He prescribed several ingredients for a remedy: an improvement in standards of teaching history in southern schools and colleges; stimulation of teaching and research through the assembling and cataloguing of historical collections, especially of works in southern history, and making them accessible to scholars regardless of their beliefs; reduction in teaching loads so that college teachers could engage in other activities; and promotion of a better southern market for books on the South. On the last ingredient Fleming wrote at length. Few Southerners bought books written by southern scholars, and fewer still read them. He had "heard numerous 'defenders of the South' condemn books they had never seen." His own works found their best market in the northern and western states; in fact, he "sold more books on Alabama in Massachusetts than in Alabama."

Fleming was certain that many of the shortcomings of United States history written in the North were the result of scant information on its southern segments. This deficiency could be diminished, he thought, "by Southern writers who will develop the history of their section and thus enable the text writers and others to obtain correct material for their work, but Southern writers cannot do this unless they receive support at home in the way of salaries, of shorter hours class work, or recognition when good work is done and last but not least some cash support in the way of purchase of books." He had noticed "a great change in the spirit of most history texts written in the North" during the past few years.

III

In evaluating Fleming's career as teacher and scholar, his brief life span is an important factor. He was fifty-eight when he died in 1932, but ill health forced retirement four years earlier. Twenty-four years of active life beyond the doctorate is a short time in which to establish an enduring reputation. It is a fact of some significance, however, that Fleming reached maturity without prolonged apprenticeship. The period of his novitiate was indeed of short duration. A meritorious article in the *American Historical Review* before he began work toward the doctorate and an exceptional dissertation that commanded immediate publication were indications that transition from student to scholar was readily accomplished. Nor did he have to grope for postdissertation research problems. A virgin field awaited exploitation.

Fleming's bibliography is tangible evidence of a busy

life. It includes ten volumes, six of them edited works; forty-four articles and collections of documents published in professional magazines; sixty contributions to dictionaries and encyclopedias; twenty-one revisions and reprintings of earlier articles; ten chapters in *The South in the Building of the Nation;* and thirty-one book reviews. His writings totaled over 5,500 pages, but about a sixth of them were chapters of forthcoming books or reprints of articles. He early formed the habit of revising and expanding monographs for republication as he discovered new evidence or matured his judgments. A few of his studies were popularized to collect a fee from nonprofessional periodicals; but his practice of reprinting articles in the same form seems questionable. Leaving reprints out of consideration, productivity reached appreciable proportions for a man who retired comparatively young and who devoted so much of his time to committee work and administrative planning.

The comprehensive dissertation, *Civil War and Reconstruction in Alabama,* was followed a year later by a new edition of *The Ku Klux Klan. Its Origin, Growth and Disbandment* (1905), published originally in 1884 by John C. Lester, a member of the Pulaski Circle, and Reverend D. L. Wilson. The value of Fleming's reprint was enhanced by a thirty-page introduction which placed the account in perspective, and by the inclusion of sundry illustrative documents. His major editorial contribution, however, was the two-volume *Documentary History of Reconstruction* (1906–1907), the continuing demand for which justified a reprinting in 1950. A milestone in documentary historiography, the volumes illustrate almost every aspect of Reconstruction history, with radical opinion dominating the first volume and conservative sentiment the second. All groups North and South have their exponents, but Negro spokesmen are so rare that their point of view is inadequately presented.

With the *Documentary History of Reconstruction* and the Alabama study completed, compilation of *The Sequel of Appomattox* was a relatively simple matter for a historian gifted with the art of condensation and mastery of expression. Few other volumes in the *Chronicles of America* equaled it in comprehensiveness or craftsmanship. The volume was, as one historian said, Fleming's "philosophy of Reconstruction." It was an interpretation by a member of the conservative school, whose work has subsequently been modified by historians who assign the Negro a more constructive role in the turbulent events of the sixties and seventies.

A less significant book, on a phase of Reconstruction history, was published near the end of Fleming's active career. *The Freedmen's Savings Bank* (1927) was a continuation of an interest that began more than twenty years before. A bifurcated article on that subject was published in the *Yale Review* during his incumbency at West Virginia University; further research yielded an expanded version and altered conclusions. Substantially correct as to facts, said a Negro critic, but *The Freedmen's Savings Bank*, like *The Sequel of Appomattox*, was predicated upon the conservative background. The *Chronicles of America* volume, in fact, provided the landscape, and the new publication therefore indicated little advancement toward revision in Fleming's thinking. In one respect it marked reversion, for it was as monographic as a master's thesis. The skilled craftsman of 1919 had lost his artistry in the interim.

Exploitation of local subjects and sources at Louisiana State University materialized in two book-length publications. General Sherman served as superintendent and professor of engineering at the State Seminary of Learning, 1860–61; a few articles on his two years as director of the school from which the university emanated preceded a

volume on *General W. T. Sherman as College President*
(1912). This assemblage of letters and other documents
provided pertinent evidence on the origins of the university, and they also portrayed the state's educational system
at the close of the ante-bellum period. Of more importance
was *Louisiana State University, 1860–1896* (1936), a fragment published posthumously. Fleming began the history
in 1909 with the intention of issuing it the following year
in commemoration of the university's fiftieth anniversary.
Eleven chapters were completed by 1911 and published at
the expense of the alumni association. Subsequently he
wrote eight more chapters, bringing the narrative to 1896,
the beginning of President Boyd's administration, and
these were incorporated with the earlier segments as a
diamond jubilee publication of the university. At the time
it was written the history was superior to most studies of
institutions of higher learning. Emphasis was, indeed, upon
administrative history; but faculty, students, and educational perspective received much more attention than college and university histories written a generation ago devoted to those subjects.

IV

These books, as well as most of Fleming's articles, were
concerned primarily with the period of restoration. Occasionally he delved into the ante-bellum and war years, as in
his dissertation, or traced an institution beyond Reconstruction, as in his history of Louisiana State University.
One major interest, however, was chiefly pre-Reconstruc-
tion, for Fleming was ambitious to write an exhaustive
biography of Jefferson Davis. He began to collect material
on the Confederate President as early as 1907 and he did
not abandon hope of finishing the task until ill health
forced his retirement in the late 1920's. In the years be-

tween 1908 and 1924 he published sixteen articles on Davis, but, following his customary procedure of reprinting papers, only ten of them were original. They dealt with such segments of Davis' career as his early life, first marriage, West Point education, religious life, camel experiment, and attitude toward the Negro. Totaling perhaps a fifth of a sizable volume, they would be only a small beginning toward a comprehensive biography.

For a decade or more Fleming worked hard at the task, ample evidence of which is available in his correspondence and other papers. To publicize his quest for Davis materials, he inserted a notice, captioned "Information Wanted About Jefferson Davis," in the New Orleans *Picayune*, October 14, 1907, which was copied by other southern newspapers. A printed circular was widely distributed, specifying the types of data he wanted: letters, diaries, scrapbooks, pamphlets, books, newspapers, pictures, relics, souvenirs, "authentic anecdotes," reminiscences, and the names of neighbors, relatives, and former slaves who could provide information. In addition to Davis letters, Fleming assembled scores of illustrations—pictures of Davis at various ages, of Mrs. Davis and other members of the family, of houses in which he lived, and of public buildings associated with the history of the Confederacy. An incomplete list of 125 correspondents, scattered widely over the United States, attests his industry in searching for data on the Confederate executive.

The circular and the newspaper publicity, as already indicated, brought numerous responses. As a modicum of miscellany: Amelia G. Gorgas of Tuscaloosa, Alabama, forwarded some letters "by registered mail." These she valued "highly, and only part from them to a biographer of Mr. Davis, who, I feel sure, will do justice to his great subject." From Mrs. Georgia P. Young of Columbus, Mississippi, came the discouraging news that an invalid neighbor "had 'stacks of letters and pictures all along through his political career,'—but—these guarded Apples of Hesperides are at present inaccessible." Josiah Gross of New Orleans, who had noticed Fleming's *Picayune* appeal, wrote that he "had numerous letters but the rats ate them, unless they are stuck away somewhere."

A generous sprinkling of Fleming's correspondents provided usable material, others offered advice as to conclusions the author should reach, and not infrequently they indicated that a contribution of documents would depend upon the biographer's interpretation of the evidence. Marie Floyd Northrop of Charlottesville, Virginia, was very explicit in stating the conditions under which she would permit the use of Davis' letters to her grandfather, the incompetent General Lucius B. Northrop. Did Fleming contemplate a "favorable" account or "a hostile attack"? "As these letters . . . go far toward vindicating my grandfather from the charges that have been made against him, you can readily understand that I should prefer that they be edited and published by the friends, rather than the enemies of Mr. Davis and my grandfather. If your work is of the hostile character indicated, I trust you, as an honorable man, to tell me so frankly; if it is not, the copies will be forthcoming as soon as they can be prepared." Fleming's "statement" of purpose was "entirely satisfactory," and the mail soon brought copies of a dozen letters.

A Dallas doctor, Frank Rainey, was "delighted" that Fleming was preparing a biography of Davis. The Texan was "intensely Southern in . . . [his] feelings," and he was convinced "that history has not dealt fairly with this truly able and worthy man," whereas there were "many histories of the tyrant Abraham Lincoln now extant, all full of extravagant falsehoods concerning him." He therefore urged Fleming "to publish no criticisms of Mr. Davis made by his enemies. If used at all let them come from those who honestly differed from him but have the manhood not to lie about him, and attempt to deceive and prejudice good people by endeavoring to make it appear that he was a traitor." Rainey then set forth his estimate of Davis and Lincoln, and the evaluation was decidedly unfavorable to Lincoln.

A resident of Montgomery, W. P. Thompson, who had learned of Fleming's project, wrote the historian that he, "personally, met Mr. Davis on four occasions during the 'hot times,'" and that he "could write . . . some *truths* and of interest." "I'll agree to do this," he continued, "conditional—I receive pay in publicity or cash." In contrast to this attempt at commercialization, Emily V. Mason of Georgetown, D. C., an aunt of Kate Mason Rowland, sent Fleming her reminiscences of Davis, dating back to the Mexican War days. "If I were not ninety two years old & if I had not 'cataracts' on both my eyes," she began her letter, "I would be tempted to talk ad infinitum on the subject."

A few of Fleming's correspondents manifested strong anti-Davis sentiments. An anonymous resident of Plaquemine, Louisiana, who identified himself as "one of the old Rebs," dipped his pen in vitriol and wrote somewhat incoherently: "Jeff Davis the traitor! When the great Emancipator Lincoln proposed to him at Fortress Monroe and would not accept—thousands of lives would have been saved and millions of money." Another anonymous writer, who resided in the national capital and whose sex and marital status cannot be doubted, penned a card to one of Fleming's friends who relayed it to the biographer: "Jeff Davis put the South *back 50 years*. If he had taken pay for the slaves we would be multi-millionaires but being crazy and a monomaniac on Secession he lost our property, fathers, sons, brothers & beaux. Many girls went through life without enjoying the pleasures of a wife or mother. He put the South back 50 years."

Perhaps these anonymous writers presented the views of fanatics. A resident of New Orleans, L. M. Pipkin, with helpful intent but hostile attitude forwarded a friend's manuscript of a "Secret Rebel History," and one of his own unpublished papers, "Could and ought the Southern Confederacy have Succeeded?" After wishing Fleming "success" in his venture, he proceeded to instruct him in the correct interpretation of his subject. He hoped the biographer had "the independence and manhood to portray the character of Mr. Davis in its true light, for I think it time to cease holding back the truth. If he committed errors, and it is known to all the Survivors in the great Civil War, that he did so in numerous instances, why not bring them out?" He had discovered the secret of Davis' present popularity. The Confederate President had dedicated his *Rise and Fall of the Confederate Government* "To the Women of the Confederacy." His object "was to enlist their sympathy—knowing that the intelligent Confederate Soldier and Civilian would and did condemn his course while Prest. of the Confederacy; and he did not reckon without his host, for now a majority of our Southern women are his misguided hero worshipers." This "old Confederate Soldier" requested "at a *very early date*" Fleming's criticism of his view. The biographer's reply was unsatisfactory. Fleming wrote that while Davis *"made many grave mistakes, there was no better 'qualified man in the South for the position, unless perhaps Lee.'"* How could the Confederate Congress be wrong? queried his correspondent. And how could all the prominent generals and many important civilian leaders be wrong? Fleming's biography was doomed to failure!

The Southerners whose documents Fleming sought and

whose counsel he received could not be expected to comprehend the fundamental task of the biographer. With
Fleming's other works before us, including the fragments
of the proposed "Jefferson Davis," it is safe to assume that
he would have sifted and weighed all the evidence carefully
and produced a critical yet sympathetic life of the Confederate President. The broad perspective in his *Civil War
and Reconstruction in Alabama* and the lucid style of his
Sequel of Appomattox are prescient indices of a well-
composed biography that would have mirrored Davis
against a social and economic as well as a political and
military background.

V

Fleming's interest in Reconstruction history and his
motive for writing it were frankly explained to conservative friends in the South. "I agree with you," he wrote to
Roulhac Hamilton in 1912, "that reconstruction is not a
delightful period for study and work. If I were teaching in
a Northern school it would not be so unpleasant, but down
South where we are so much of the remnants of the thing
the work is quite unpleasant." Nevertheless, as early as
1900 he sought priority in the field, and expressed to Owen
a hope that "no one will infringe on Ala." A month later
he included in a letter to Owen one of the few ungenerous
statements that came from his pen. There must have been
an element of jealousy when he inquired how his correspondent liked William G. Brown's recent article on "The
Ku Klux Movement," a really superior piece of work. "We
have read him out of the party here," said Fleming. In
1904 he began to reprint some Reconstruction documents.
Among his reasons for doing so, set down in a letter to
another Dunning student who was still at Columbia, he
stressed a desire "to occupy the unworked field to the ex-

clusion of such d—— f——'s as [Paul Leland] Haworth
. . . who might take a similar notion. I consider myself
better qualified to do the work than a New Englander or a
wild Westerner." And, as we have already seen, he would
write Reconstruction history to correct the "false impression" of postwar events which northern historians had
recorded.

It was Fleming's intention when he began his dissertation to limit investigation to the Reconstruction era of
Alabama history. He soon decided that it would be necessary to consider the war period also, for an understanding
of the state's internal problems in wartime was requisite to
an appreciation of the course of restoration, and these in
turn required a foundation in ante-bellum history. The
study represented five or six times as much work as many
of the dissertations accepted at Hopkins before 1900. It
was a new departure in another respect: social and economic history had received meager attention by Fleming's
predecessors and most of his contemporaries; yet almost
half of his eight-hundred-page volume is devoted to social,
industrial, religious, and educational history. Primarily
a study of the local scene, the work does not ignore the
national picture.

More than most historians of recent eras, Fleming carried on correspondence with surviving participants in the
events he investigated. The war and Reconstruction periods
yielded a sizable group of "contemporaries." Fleming was
particularly anxious to have both sides of controversial
questions before him as he wrote, and he therefore sought
information from radicals and their descendants as well
as from conservatives. Some of his correspondents furnished
important documents or clues to their location; others
penned their reminiscences; and still others counseled
the historian on how he should interpret events. A sampling of this correspondence may serve to indicate how con-

temporaries viewed the period a quarter of a century after the restoration of home rule in Alabama.

In an effort to discover the radical point of view and documentary evidence in possession of radicals, Fleming wrote to several members of that group, among them Paul Strobach, Joseph C. Manning, and Asa E. Stratton. Strobach lived in Spokane, Washington, in 1902, but he had resided in Alabama from 1865 until 1885. "I was prominently connected with the reconstruction," he replied in answer to Fleming's request for information, "and am perhaps the best informed man about all of its phases in the country, having been a member of the Legislature, High Sheriff of Montgomery during the Ku-Klux period, United States Marshal and Member of Congress elected, but counted out." Assembling data for the historian would require more time than he devoted to magazine articles for which he received from twenty-five to fifty dollars apiece. "Please write me how much you are willing to pay," he proposed, "and I will let you know if the terms are satisfactory." Fleming was willing to compensate the former carpetbagger for information. In discussing Republican factionalism in the election of 1874, he appended as a footnote: "A few years ago Strobach offered to tell me all about his political career in exchange for $50, but died before he could begin the account."

Less acquisitive was Manning, of Alexander City, Alabama, who suggested that Fleming correspond with John Anthony Winston Smith, lily-white Republican candidate for governor in 1902, whose father, William H. Smith, was a Republican governor of Alabama during the Reconstruction. He should also write to Lewis E. Parsons, son of another Republican governor, who was "a really great and good man." From Parsons, Fleming could "get the straight and honest and consistent detail of interesting facts that you seek from a true Republican of ability—without any prefixes." If he wanted a carpetbagger's point of view, he should consult Judge Asa E. Stratton. Fleming had already written to Stratton, who thought an objective history of Alabama Reconstruction would serve a useful purpose, "for partisan misrepresentations have done much to retard the restoration of the South, and to keep out of power republicans in this section." Stratton was a Confederate soldier "without democratic feelings." If Fleming desired, he would put his recollections on paper, "which you can make such use of as you see proper."

Frequent footnote recognition of extradocumentary sources is no adequate measure of Fleming's obligation to oral and written testimony of the period's contemporaries, or, for that matter, of his own firsthand knowledge derived from surviving mores. A few citations, however, may serve to illustrate reliance upon correspondence and interviews. "I am indebted to old soldiers for descriptions and of conditions in north and west Alabama" is a typical entry, and so is his acknowledgment, "My chief source of information in regard to the common schools during the war has been the accounts of persons who were teachers and pupils in the schools." Other footnotes contain such expressions as "conversations with various negroes and whites," "accounts of negroes and whites who were at the polls," or simply "oral accounts and personal observation." Sometimes he identified his informant, as in the note, "I am especially indebted to Professor L. D. Miller, Jacksonville, Ala., for many details concerning the Loyal Leagues. He made inquiries for me of people who knew the facts." Wherever possible Fleming verified reminiscences against contemporary documents. The recollections of General Wager Swayne, Freedmen's Bureau assistant commissioner for Alabama, were correct, he found, even though a third of a century had intervened since the stirring events of Reconstruction days.

It is apparent that Fleming was no "arm-chair" historian, solely dependent upon printed and manuscript records preserved in libraries and archives. For these standard sources he made diligent search and, at least as far as published documents were concerned, just about exhausted the material on his subject. One cannot peruse his *Civil War and Reconstruction in Alabama* without appreciating the intimate and personalized character of the narrative. Fleming's correspondence and interviews with Alabamians whose recollections of the years 1860–75 were still vivid in their memories yielded answers to questions which the historian could not ask of inanimate records; and a keen perception of life and institutions in his own day provided a spirit of the times applicable to a past which still survived in most of its fundamental attributes.

Fleming closed his Alabama study by placing in juxtaposition rival views of Reconstruction. One of them stressed constructive accomplishments of the congressional program and resulting progress of the Negro race: civil rights, theoretical guarantees of suffrage, political and religious independence and economic freedom, public schools for both races, removal of the "baleful influence" of conservative whites, and justification of "the 'political hell' through which the whites passed" as "necessary discipline." Fleming's findings refuted these claims: he concluded that "any rights or privileges or advantages" possessed by Alabama Negroes in 1900 had been freely "offered by the native whites" in 1865–66.

While neither view is correct, the shortcomings of Fleming's *Civil War and Reconstruction in Alabama* are readily apparent a half century later. He could not free himself from the conservative milieu in which he grew up. Surface irritation, injudicious expressions, sympathy for the white South, and inability to assign a measure of credit to other groups were attributes that prevented his work from ap-

proaching objectivity or reaching definitiveness. Conservatives were assured of a sympathetic hearing before his
court; the testimony of radicals would be heard, but the
court would determine its admissibility as evidence and
judge its significance in the final verdict. And yet Du Bois'
appraisal of the book as "pure propaganda" attributes an
erroneous motive. Fleming was endeavoring to correct
misconceptions which pervaded Reconstruction history in
his generation. He wrote in the spirit and atmosphere of a
region that nursed grievances against government and
society. He could easily convince himself that he was a
critical historian striving for objectivity. As he often said
to fellow historians of the South, southern laymen were
unwilling to accept as valid the work of their own trained
historians. Occupying a position slightly to the left of conservatism, his concessions to an unorthodox view, meager
as they may seem today, gave him a sense of impartiality.

How would the present-day critical scholar modify
Fleming's *Sequel of Appomattox* to make it acceptable to
revisionists? With the author's southernism in attention's
focus, the writer has reread the "Chronicle of the Reunion
of the States" against the background of enlightened studies
published during the last thirty-five years. That Fleming
still sympathized with white Southerners, that he included
some quotations and a few statements of his own that made
the Negro appear ridiculous, and that he approved the
North's recantation are quite obvious. Like most histories
written by serious scholars, however, the greater part of
the *Sequel of Appomattox* consists of factual data the
validity of which no one would dispute. A revisionist at
mid-twentieth century could rewrite thirty of the three
hundred pages and therein correct factual errors, delete
unfortunate expressions, eliminate statements glorifying
the white race, and appraise judiciously the roles of all

political groups and agencies. If the writer's estimation that the redrafting of lines totaling a tenth of the study would bring conformity with revisionist thought, the volume made some permanent contribution to Reconstruction historiography. If he reads critically, one may still profit from its pages. Unfortunately, the imperfections as well as the merits are a part of the record; hence the necessity for a new synthesis that will retain its solid worth and expunge its defects.

VI

Failure to appreciate positive contributions of Negroes to the Reconstruction era and overcensure of their negative role led inevitably to reappraisals. The first significant protest against conservatism was voiced by W. E. B. Du Bois in a paper on "Reconstruction and Its Benefits," presented at the annual meeting of the American Historical Association in 1909. The premise that the Negro in politics was chiefly responsible for the period's adversities did his race an injustice, he asserted, for evils would have followed the war if there had been no Negroes in the South. If white Southerners had been permitted to control restored states on the basis of the Black Codes, Negro status would have approximated slavery. Admitting the evils of radical control, Du Bois assigned a large measure of responsibility for bad government to members of the white race and insisted that new social legislation, free public schools, and democratic government were positive accomplishments of Negro rule. These views created a mild sensation, for already the guild had largely acquiesced in the Dunning interpretation of the war's aftermath. He and his preceptor, Burgess, in common with most scholars of the period, had accepted the doctrine that the Negro was innately inferior, and a process of Reconstruction that subordinated Caucasians was "entirely unnatural, ruinous, and utterly demoralizing and barbarizing to both races."

Another landmark in the origin of protest occurred in 1915 with the establishment in Washington of the Association for the Study of Negro Life and History and the inauguration the following year of the *Journal of Negro History* with Carter Woodson as editor. Revisors of the conservative view now had a scholarly periodical to supplement book-length studies in presenting an affirmative as well as a refutory case for a group that had few spokesmen in the period following restoration of "home rule" in the South. As might be expected, positive and negative approaches were sometimes militant and overzealous. The Dunning studies, written to prove the Negro's incapacity for participation in government and to justify methods used to overthrow Reconstruction regimes, said one contributor, were "worthless" because authors selected facts to "establish their point of view" and ignored evidence that disproved it. The periodical's pages bristled with censorious appraisals of the conservative school bemingled with considerable praiseworthy detachment.

But the severest critic of conservative Reconstruction literature was Du Bois, whose *Black Reconstruction* surveyed the troublous sixties and seventies and concluded with a chapter on "The Propaganda of History." Dunning and his students wrote according to a pattern: "endless sympathy with the white South"; "ridicule, contempt or silence for the Negro"; and "a judicial attitude towards the North, which concludes that the North under great misapprehension did a grievous wrong, but eventually saw its mistake and retreated." In Du Bois' view, Fleming selected source materials for his *Documentary History of Reconstruction* to support a thesis; his Alabama study was "pure propaganda." On the other hand, he classified Fleming's *Freemen's Savings Bank* and his article on "Deportation and Colonization" among monographs whose "authors seek the facts in certain narrow definite fields and in most cases do not ignore the truth as to Negroes."

The literature of controversy is always confusing, the more so because many who write it speak with too much assurance. Theoretically, "scientific" training divests the student of influences that emanate from lineage and locale and immunizes him against chance aberrations that warp the mind and unfit it for objective thought. Unfortunately, the human equation is always present in the battle between objectivity and subjectivity, and the victory of the former is seldom complete. Clash of conclusion in controversial literature leads inevitably to assignment of motive to those who disagree. Conservative historians of Reconstruction employed the structure of "scientific" history, revisionists admitted, but the purpose was often a shield to camouflage propaganda. With similar phraseology and intent, Fleming asserted that a revisionist combined "modern scientific method with the bias of ancient prejudice." Book reviews and annotated bibliographies endeavored to consign rival thinkers to oblivion by the application of such epithets as "apologist for slavery," "apologist for the Negro," "apologist for conservatism," "apologist for radicalism." Terse judgments wrap a neat package but leave much merit unsheathed.

Historiography comes of age each generation—for that generation. In the period between the 1890's and the 1920's, Reconstruction historiography reached maturity in the writings of William A. Dunning and his students, particularly Fleming. An interpretation of a period or a movement is seldom wholly acceptable, however, to any generation of scholars. Divergent thought arises to challenge conclusions generally held valid, and the transition to a new interpretation begins before the old is firmly established. Historiography is seldom static. The dynamics of history are always present to inspire a search for new emphasis and new meaning—and to leave a cumulative quality in its wake. Like the civilization history records, it carries forward much that is old as it advances to new frontiers. Oberholtzer and Rhodes, Dunning and Fleming still live in publications that seem very fresh and modern in 1955. It is not surprising to find that much factual information reappears in successive histories; it is startling to discover that concepts and ideas and interpretations attributed to recent scholars were the possession of an earlier generation's historians.

The fact remains that historiography is innovative as well as cumulative; as innovation it is neologic as well as neoteric. In the last quarter century Simkins and Woody, Beale and Wharton, Du Bois and Bond, and a dozen others have contributed to a new concept of the tragic era, although as yet it has not reached fruition. Eventually someone with mastery of data, keen perception, and objective intent will provide an interpretive synthesis that will supersede Fleming's effort. It will weigh carefully the component parts of the old philosophy before discarding them. It will avoid the sensationalism of revolutionary dynamics to provoke a hearing. Sensationalism in history destroys effectiveness.

Fleming's contribution to Reconstruction historiography must be evaluated, of course, not only by standards and conclusions prevailing in the 1950's; it must also be measured in terms of the climate of opinion in which he labored. Judging his works by concepts of the era in which he wrote, they seem worthy of acclaim. Their comprehensive framework is a permanent legacy; the conservative mosaic a necessary step in the development of an accurate portrayal.

Essay on Authorities

The Southern Avenue to Now

THE STORY of a developing historical scholarship in the South is widely scattered in private correspondence and in professional journals. The manuscript collections listed in later segments of sources illumine many of the origins of historical activities; national and regional reviews and state historical society quarterlies provide ample evidence of worthy workmanship. An exhaustive bibliography would include hundreds of articles relating to sundry aspects of the guild's achievements and the means by which they were attained; here only a few of the more important ones will be listed.

A significant survey of one facet of southern historical scholarship is presented in Fletcher M. Green, "Writing and Research in Southern History," South Carolina Historical Association *Proceedings, 1942* (Columbia, 1942), [3–17]. Active participation of J. G. de Roulhac Hamilton in sundry aspects of the region's historical advancement gives weight to "History in the South—A Retrospect of Half a Century," *North Carolina Historical Review* (Raleigh), XXXI (April, 1954), 173–81. The story to the end of the nineteenth century is well told in E. Merton Coulter, "What the South Has Done About Its History," *Journal of Southern History* (Baton Rouge, Lexington), II (February, 1936), 3–28. An important recent segment is treated in David M. Potter, "An Appraisal of Fifteen Years of the Journal of Southern History, 1935–1949," *Journal of Southern History*, XVI (February, 1950), 25–32;

122 THE SOUTH LIVES IN HISTORY

and in H. C. Nixon, "Paths to the Past: The Presidential Addresses of the Southern Historical Association," *Journal of Southern History*, XVI, 33–39. Charles S. Sydnor, "Historical Activities in Mississippi in the Nineteenth Century," *Journal of Southern History*, III (May, 1937), 139–60, is a valuable summary of a state's struggles to initiate and maintain historical projects. The preservation of original materials is discussed in Philip M. Hamer, "The Records of Southern History," *Journal of Southern History*, V (February, 1939), 3–17; and in J. G. de Roulhac Hamilton, "Three Centuries of Southern Records, 1607–1907," *Journal of Southern History*, X (February, 1944), 3–36. Influences that affected the region's historiography in the last decade are treated in Clement Eaton, "Recent Trends in the Writing of Southern History," *Louisiana Historical Quarterly* (New Orleans), XXXVIII (April, 1955), 26–42.

Approaching the problem at the state level, the *North Carolina Historical Review* published a series of articles on the preservation of history in southern commonwealths: Lyon G. Tyler, "Preservation of Virginia History," III (October, 1926), 529–38; J. G. de Roulhac Hamilton, "The Preservation of North Carolina History," IV (January, 1927), 3–21; A. S. Salley, Jr., "Preservation of South Carolina History," IV (April, 1927), 145–57; Theodore H. Jack, "The Preservation of Georgia History," IV (July, 1927), 239–51; James A. Robertson, "The Preservation of Florida History," IV (October, 1927), 351–65; Mitchell B. Garrett, "The Preservation of Alabama History," V (January, 1928), 3–19; William H. Weathersby, "The Preservation of Mississippi History," V (April, 1928), 141–50; David Y. Thomas, "The Preservation of Arkansas History," V (July, 1928), 263–74; Grace King, "The Preservation of Louisiana History," V (October, 1928), 363–71; Charles W. Ramsdell, "The Preservation of Texas History," VI (January, 1929),

1–16; and Philip M. Hamer, "The Preservation of Tennessee History," VI (April, 1929), 127–39.

In assembling the chapter, however, the writer drew heavily upon his own previous articles: "History of the South in Colleges and Universities, 1925–1926," *Historical Outlook* (Philadelphia), XVII (November, 1926), 319–22; "The South Lives in History: A Decade of Historical Investigation," *Historical Outlook,* XXIII (April, 1932), 153–63; "A Half Century of Southern Historical Scholarship," *Journal of Southern History,* XI (February, 1945), 3–32; "William P. Trent as a Historian of the South," *Journal of Southern History,* XV (May, 1949), 151–77; "William Garrott Brown: Literary Historian and Essayist," *Journal of Southern History,* XII (August, 1946), 313–44; "Herbert B. Adams and Southern Historical Scholarship at the Johns Hopkins University," *Maryland Historical Magazine* (Baltimore), XLII (March, 1947), 1–20; "John Spencer Bassett as a Historian of the South," *North Carolina Historical Review,* XXV (July, 1948), 289–317; "The Negro in the Thinking and Writing of John Spencer Bassett," *North Carolina Historical Review,* XXV (October, 1948), 427–41; and the trilogy, "Some Pioneer Alabama Historians": "George Petrie," *Alabama Review* (Tuscaloosa), I (July, 1948), 164–79; "Walter L. Fleming," *Alabama Review,* I (October, 1948), 261–78; and "Thomas M. Owen," *Alabama Review,* II (January, 1949), 45–62.

William E. Dodd

The correspondence of Dodd and his contemporaries provides illuminating information on the development of the historian and the status of the guild in his generation. The copious Dodd Papers, Manuscripts Division, Library of Congress, Washington, D.C., were still in private possession when the writer used them in the spring of 1945. Thanks to Mrs. Alfred K. (Martha Dodd) Stern, he was given access to the hundred filing boxes relating to her father's career as historian while they were stored at the Stern home near Ridgefield, Connecticut. A few items, dating back to the 1890's, yielded notes on Dodd's early life—his candidacy for West Point and examinations for teacher certificates; but the papers consist mainly of correspondence with historians, politicians, and publishers. One of the most interesting items is a long memorandum of his visit at the White House with President Theodore Roosevelt early in 1908.

Among the scores of historians with whom Dodd corresponded were Charles Francis Adams, Herbert Baxter Adams, Charles H. Ambler, James C. Ballagh, Frederic Bancroft, Eugene C. Barker, Kemp P. Battle, Charles A. Beard, Albert J. Beveridge, Herbert Eugene Bolton, William K. Boyd, R. D. W. Connor, Avery Craven, William A. Dunning, Carl R. Fish, Walter Lynwood Fleming, Douglas Southall Freeman, Ralph H. Gabriel, George P. Garrison, Albert B. Hart, Charles H. Haskins, Archibald Henderson, J. Franklin Jameson, Allen Johnson, John H. Latané, Andrew C. McLaughlin, Colyer Meriwether, Albert B. Moore, Frank L. Owsley, George Petrie, Charles W. Ramsdell, Yates Snowden, H. Morse Stephens, William P. Trent, Frederick Jackson Turner, Lyon G. Tyler, and Laura A. White.

Of secondary importance but nonetheless significant to an understanding of Dodd's concept of democracy was his correspondence with political figures. This began as early as 1907 and reached considerable volume in the period after World War I. Among his political correspondents, some of whom wrote on historical subjects, were William Jennings Bryan, Henry G. Connor, James M. Cox, Josephus Daniels, John W. Davis, Edward M. House, Claude Kitchin,

William G. McAdoo, Henry Morgenthau, Theodore Roosevelt, Daniel C. Roper, and Woodrow Wilson.

The range of his letter writing is also indicated by correspondence with such college and university administrators as Edwin A. Alderman, George H. Denny, Robert M. Hutchins, Harry P. Judson, and Charles D. McIver; and with such publicists and journalists as Herbert Croly, Curtis N. Hitchcock, Arthur W. Page, Walter H. Page, Clarence Poe, and Oswald G. Villard.

The manuscript collections of other historians also yielded correspondence with Dodd: Herbert Baxter Adams Papers, Johns Hopkins University Library, Baltimore; John Spencer Bassett Papers, in possession of Mrs. Bassett, Northampton, Massachusetts, when the writer used them in the fall of 1944; William K. Boyd Papers, Manuscript Division, Duke University Library, Durham; Henry G. Connor Papers, R. D. W. Connor Papers, and J. G. de Roulhac Hamilton Papers, Southern Historical Collection, University of North Carolina Library, Chapel Hill; Ulrich B. Phillips Papers, transcripts in possession of the writer; and Yates Snowden Papers, South Caroliniana Library, University of South Carolina, Columbia. The "Review Correspondence" and other American Historical Association Papers, Manuscripts Division, Library of Congress, are replete with information on historians who contributed to the *American Historical Review* or engaged in association activities.

After Dodd's death in 1940 his unpublished diary for the years 1916 to 1925, a few other personal papers, chiefly outlines or drafts of speeches and lecture notes, and his library of some 1,750 volumes, periodicals, reprints, maps, and scrapbooks of clippings were given to Randolph-Macon College, Ashland, Virginia. They are housed in the Dodd Room of the college library. The significant portion of the diary, 1916–20, was edited by W. Alexander

Mabry and published in *The John P. Branch Historical Papers of Randolph-Macon College* (Ashland), N. S., II (March, 1953), [1]–86. The manuscript diary is in four books, but the entries in Book III are very sporadic, and Book IV is mainly a record of speaking engagements for 1925 with an occasional diary entry. The content relates to such matters as historical activities at Chicago and elsewhere, departmental and university affairs, social engagements, World War I, and farm life at Round Hill, Virginia.

The Southern Historical Collection at the University of North Carolina has a small assemblage of Dodd Papers, 1911–23. It consists of copies of letters from Theodore Roosevelt and Woodrow Wilson to Dodd relating to the historian's publications and speeches.

The writer is indebted to Professor Theodore F. Note of Virginia Polytechnic Institute, Blacksburg, December 7, 1951, for valuable information on that college's offerings during the period that Dodd was a student there, and for transcripts from the *Catalogue of the Virginia Agricultural and Mechanical College and Polytechnic Institute, 1895–96* (Lynchburg, 1895), describing courses in history; and to Clarice Slusher, registrar, October 6, 1951, for a transcript of Dodd's record at the institute.

Other requests for information on the historian's early life yielded less tangible results, but the writer gratefully acknowledges helpful letters from Christopher C. Crittenden, director of the Department of Archives and History, Raleigh, November 30, December 31, 1951; James O. Waters, principal of Clayton Public Schools, North Carolina, n.d. (1950); and W. A. Young, superintendent of Glen Alpine Schools, North Carolina, September 26, 1951. Search for assistance from relatives brought an informative letter from Dodd's brother, E. D. Dodd, Fuquay Springs, North Carolina, February 28, 1952, who wrote that William studied until late at night after working on the farm from sunrise to sunset.

Dodd's teaching programs at Randolph-Macon College and at the University of Chicago are available in *Catalogue of Randolph-Macon College, 1900–1908* (Lynchburg, 1900–1908); and in the University of Chicago *Annual Register, 1907–30* (Chicago, 1908–31). Some extracurricular historical activities at Randolph-Macon College are recorded in *The John P. Branch Historical Papers of Randolph-Macon College*, 5 vols. (Richmond, 1901–18). The first two volumes, 1901–1904 and 1905–1908, appeared under Dodd's editorship.

Jack K. Williams, "A Bibliography of the Printed Writings of William Edward Dodd," *North Carolina Historical Review*, XXX (January, 1953), 72–85, like Mabry's "Professor William E. Dodd's Diary, 1916–1920," appeared after the writer had completed research, but it has served as a check list of the historian's important publications. While the bibliography is inaccurate and incomplete, omitting articles and reviews published in newspapers and a few periodicals and all unpublished articles, little of consequence will be missed if the researcher depends entirely upon the items it includes.

Dodd's books, other than edited works and co-operative texts, follow in the order of publication: *Thomas Jefferson's Rückkehr zur Politik, 1796* (Leipzig, 1899); *The Life of Nathaniel Macon* (Raleigh, 1903); *Jefferson Davis* (Philadelphia, 1907); *Statesmen of the Old South; or From Radicalism to Conservative Revolt* (New York, 1911); *Expansion and Conflict* (Boston, 1915); *The Cotton Kingdom; A Chronicle of the Old South* (New Haven, 1919); *Woodrow Wilson and His Work* (Garden City, 1920); *Lincoln or Lee; Comparison and Contrast of the Two Greatest Leaders in the War Between the States. The Narrow and Accidental*

Margins of Success (New York, 1928); *The Old South; Struggles for Democracy* (New York, 1937); *Ambassador Dodd's Diary, 1933–1938* (New York, 1941), edited by William E. Dodd, Jr., and Martha Dodd, with an introduction by Charles A. Beard. In the period 1928–34 Dodd collaborated with other historians in writing five textbooks at the elementary, high school, and college levels; some years earlier he co-operated with his Chicago colleagues, Andrew C. McLaughlin, Marcus W. Jernegan, and Arthur P. Scott, in compiling *Source Problems in United States History* (New York, 1918).

The Wilson biography prompted the President's widow to select Dodd as the appropriate historian to collaborate with Ray Stannard Baker in editing *The Public Papers of Woodrow Wilson, Authorized Edition*. The work appeared in three series: *College and State, Educational, Literary and Political Papers (1875–1913)*, 2 vols. (New York, 1925); *The New Democracy; Presidential Messages, Addresses, and Other Papers (1913–1917)*, 2 vols. (New York, 1926); *War and Peace; Presidential Messages, Addresses, and Public Papers (1917–1924)*, 2 vols. (New York, 1927).

A generous sampling of Dodd's shorter works must suffice. The historian's interest in American political leaders manifested itself in articles as well as in books. He contributed several collections of documents and articles, chiefly on Leven Powell, John Cooper Granbery, John Taylor of Caroline, Thomas Ritchie, Spencer Roane, and John Marshall, to the *Branch Historical Papers*, I–II (1901–1908). More specifically, he published "Tom Paine," *American Mercury* (New York), XXI (December, 1930), 477–83; "Napoleon Breaks Thomas Jefferson," *American Mercury*, V (July, 1925), 303–13; "George Washington, Nationalist," American Historical Association *Annual Report*, 1932 (Washington, 1934), 133–48; "Chief Justice Marshall and Virginia, 1813–1821," *American Historical Review* (New

York), XII (July, 1907), 776–87; "The Place of Nathaniel Macon in Southern History," *American Historical Review*, VII (July, 1902), 663–75; and "Robert J. Walker, Imperialist," Chicago Literary Club *Papers* (Chicago, 1914), 7–40.

Jackson, Lincoln, and Wilson were favorite subjects with Dodd, especially in contributions to popular magazines. Two articles on the great Democrat of the 1830's appeared in *Century Magazine* (New York): "The Making of Andrew Jackson; All Things Worked Together for Good to Old Hickory," CXI (March, 1926), 531–38; and "Andrew Jackson and His Enemies, And the Great Noise They Made in the World," CXI (April, 1926), 734–45. The essays in *Lincoln or Lee* appeared contemporaneously in *Century Magazine:* "The Rise of Abraham Lincoln; Lifting the Burdens from the Shoulders of All Men," CXIII (March, 1927), 569–84; "Lincoln or Lee: No Peace Without Victory in a War-Mad World," CXIII (April, 1927), 661–73; and "Lincoln's Last Struggle And the End of His Long and Toilsome Course," CXIV (May, 1927), 46–61. He also published "Lincoln's Last Struggle—Victory?" Lincoln Centennial Association *Papers* (Springfield, Illinois, 1927), 49–98; and "Lincoln's Dilemma," M. Llewellyn Raney *et al., If Lincoln Had Lived* (Chicago, 1935), 43–58. Two articles on Wilson appeared during the war: "The Social and Economic Background of Woodrow Wilson," *Journal of Political Economy* (Chicago), XXV (March, 1917), 261–85; and "President Wilson and the World Peace," *Nation* (New York), CVII (November 9, 1918), 557–58. A segment of *Woodrow Wilson and His Work,* "President Wilson, His Treaty, and His Reward," appeared in *World's Work* (New York), XXXIX (March, 1920), 440–47, but, according to Dodd, on condition that it be accompanied by William M. Fullerton's article, "The Bewilderment of America," as an antidote. The publication of the biography was followed by other articles on the war

president, among them "Wilson and the American Tradition," *Pacific Review* (Seattle), I (March, 1921), 576–81;
"Wilsonism," *Political Science Quarterly* (New York),
XXXVIII (March, 1923), 115–32; "Woodrow Wilson—Ten
Years After," *Contemporary Review* (New York), CXXXV
(January, 1929), 26–38; and a pamphlet, *Woodrow Wilson,
1918–1920, and the World Situation, 1938* (Philadelphia,
1938). Several other articles, published in periodicals and
newspapers, had a Wilson flavor.

The central theme of many of Dodd's writings, whether
books or articles, was democracy; interest in that aspect of
American life appeared in several items already listed.
Among other articles with that thesis are three concerned
with education: "Democracy and Learning," *Nation*,
LXXXIX (November 4, 1909), 430–31; "Democracy and
the University," *Nation*, CI (October 14, 1915), 463–65;
and "The University and the Totalitarian State," *Educational Record* (Washington), XIX (July, 1938), 312–22. Of
more significance are "The Struggle for Democracy in the
United States," *International Journal of Ethics* (Chicago),
XXVIII (July, 1918), 465–84; "The Converging Democracies of England and America," North Carolina State Literary and Historical Association *Proceedings,* 1918 (Raleigh,
1919), 85–98, which also appeared in slightly abbreviated
form as "The Converging Democracies," *Yale Review* (New
Haven), N. S., VIII (April, 1919), 449–65; "The Dilemma
of Democracy in the United States," *Virginia Quarterly
Review* (Charlottesville), I (October, 1925), 350–63; and
"Shall Our Farmers Become Peasants," *Century*, CXVI
(May, 1928), 30–44.

As a sampling of miscellanea, see "Another View of Our
Educational Progress," *South Atlantic Quarterly* (Durham),
II (October, 1903), 325–33; "Some Difficulties of the His-
tory Teacher in the South," *South Atlantic Quarterly*, III
(April, 1904), 117–22; "History and Patriotism," *South*

Atlantic Quarterly, XII (April, 1913), 109–21; "Robert E. Lee and Reconstruction," *South Atlantic Quarterly*, IV (January, 1905), 63–70; "Freedom of Speech in the South," *Nation*, LXXXIV (April 25, 1907), 383–84; "The Status of History in Southern Education," *Nation*, LXXV (August 7, 1902), 109–11; "The Declaration of Independence," *Virginia Quarterly Review*, II (July, 1926), 334–49; "Virginia Takes the Road to Revolution," Carl Becker, J. M. Clark, and William E. Dodd, *The Spirit of '76 and Other Essays* (Washington, 1927), [99]–135; "The Great Loyalty in America," *Historical Outlook*, X (October, 1919), 363–67; "The Social Philosophy of the Old South," *American Journal of Sociology* (Chicago), XXIII (May, 1918), 735–46; "Economic Interpretation of American History," *Journal of Political Economy*, XXIV (May, 1916), 489–95; "Have the Scientists Done a Better Job?" *Christian Century* (Chicago), XLVI, Pt. I (January 31, 1929), 138–41; "Karl Lamprecht and Kulturgeschichte," *Popular Science Monthly* (New York), LXIII (September, 1903), 418–24; "The Fight for the Northwest, 1860," *American Historical Review*, XVI (July, 1911), 774–88; "Profitable Fields of Investigation in American History, 1815–1860," *American Historical Review*, XVIII (April, 1913), 522–36; "The Emergence of the First Social Order in the United States," *American Historical Review*, XL (January, 1935), 217–31.

Many of Dodd's articles published in popular magazines and a few that found lodgment in professional journals were of "New History" vintage, written in a presentist atmosphere; his contributions to dictionaries and encyclopedias were strictly orthodox. His articles in Julian A. C. Chandler *et al.* (eds.), *The South in the Building of the Nation*, 12 vols. (Richmond, 1909), were concerned with economic thought and history; those in Andrew C. McLaughlin and Albert B. Hart (eds.), *Cyclopedia of American Government*, 3 vols. (New York, 1914); Allen Johnson,

Dumas Malone, and Harris E. Starr (eds.), *Dictionary of American Biography,* 21 vols. and index (New York, 1928–44); Edwin R. A. Seligman (ed.), *Encyclopaedia of the Social Sciences,* 15 vols. (New York, 1930–35); and *Encyclopedia Americana,* 30 vols. (New York, 1949), were mainly biographical sketches of southern political figures. His numerous book reviews appeared in the *American Historical Review,* the *Virginia Quarterly Review,* the *South Atlantic Quarterly,* the *North Carolina Historical Review,* the *Mississippi Valley Historical Review* (Cedar Rapids), the *Journal of Modern History* (Chicago), the *New England Quarterly* (Baltimore), and in sundry New York and Chicago newspapers.

There are brief notes on Dodd's career as a historian in Michael Kraus, *The Writing of American History* (Norman, 1953); Thomas J. Pressly, *Americans Interpret Their Civil War* (Princeton, 1954); and Wendell H. Stephenson, "A Half Century of Southern Historical Scholarship," *Journal of Southern History,* XI (February, 1945), 3–32. An obituary notice appeared in the *American Historical Review,* XLV (April, 1940), 756–57. Three of Dodd's former colleagues at the University of Chicago contributed addresses to the May, 1940, issue of the *University of Chicago Magazine* (Chicago): Avery Craven, "As Teacher," 7–8; Charles E. Merriam, "As Statesman," 8–9; and Marcus W. Jernegan, "As Historian," 10, 27. The introduction to *Ambassador Dodd's Diary,* by Charles A. Beard, is a helpful appraisal; and Herman Ausubel, *Historians and Their Craft: A Study of the Presidential Addresses of the American Historical Association, 1884–1945* (New York, 1950), evaluates the historian's article, "The Emergence of the First Social Order in the United States." The ambassadorship to Germany is only incidentally a part of the present study; the *Diary* of those years yields significant insight into the ambassador's personification of democracy in Berlin as well as a few notes on his Virginia farm. Valuable for an understanding of the diplomatic years are Franklin L. Ford, "Three Observers in Berlin: Rumbold, Dodd, and François-Poncet," in Gordon Craig and Felix Gilbert (eds.), *The Diplomats, 1919–1939* (Princeton, 1953); Martha Dodd Stern, *Through Embassy Eyes* (New York, 1939); and J. Claybrook Lewis, "William E. Dodd, Democratic Diplomat," *Branch Historical Papers*, N. S., II (March, 1953), [87]–140.

Ulrich B. Phillips

By courtesy of Mrs. Phillips, the writer was given access to the surviving papers of Ulrich B. Phillips. Three sets of transcripts were made, one of which the writer retained; the others were presented to the Agricultural History Society and the Southern Historical Collection of the University of North Carolina Library. Among Phillips' correspondents were John B. Andrews, James B. Angell, David Rankin Barbee, Chauncey S. Boucher, William Cabell Bruce, Nicholas Murray Butler, William H. Carpenter, Avery Craven, William E. Dodd, William A. Dunning, Richard T. Ely, Frank D. Fackenthal, Carl R. Fish, Worthington C. Ford, Fairfax Harrison, Charles H. Haskins, DuBose Heyward, J. Franklin Jameson, Allen Johnson, Alvin Johnson, Achille Loria, Andrew C. McLaughlin, Dumas Malone, Albert R. Newsome, Wallace Notestein, John M. Parker, George Foster Peabody, David M. Potter, Prentiss B. Reed, Edwin R. A. Seligman, Charles Seymour, Justin H. Smith, Nathaniel W. Stephenson, Helen L. Sumner, Frederick Jackson Turner, Carl Van Doren, Theodore L. Van Norden, Bell I. Wiley, James Southall Wilson, and Carl Wittke.

The Phillips Papers also contain considerable correspondence with publishing houses; the largest parcel is concerned with arrangements for the publication of *Plantation and Frontier*. More than sixty pages of proposed designs and correspondence—chiefly with Ely, Sumner, and Andrews—were required in Phillips' case alone before publishers, directors, and editors approved format of front-matter pages and spines and distribution of credit for the co-operative ten-volume *A Documentary History of American Industrial Society* (Cleveland, 1910–11).

A small parcel of some forty Phillips letters, 1903, 1908–10, transferred from the large collection of George J. Baldwin Papers, Southern Historical Collection, University of North Carolina Library, are especially valuable for Phillips' counsel in efforts to reorganize the Georgia Historical Society in 1903 and his early research and publication interests. The Bassett, Boyd, Dodd, Hamilton, Snowden, and American Historical Association Papers, already listed, contain Phillips letters. Other collections in which Phillips correspondence is available include: Eugene C. Barker Letters, Archives Collection, University of Texas, Austin; Philip Alexander Bruce Papers, Manuscripts Division, University of Virginia Library, Charlottesville; Fairfax Harrison Papers, William and Mary College Library, Williamsburg; Departmental Correspondence (chiefly Thomas M. Owen Papers), Alabama Department of Archives and History, Montgomery; Maps and Manuscripts Room (other Owen correspondence), Alabama Department of Archives and History; Charles W. Ramsdell Papers, in possession of Mrs. Ramsdell, Plainview, Texas.

Supplementing transcripts of Phillips' records from the registrars' offices of Tulane University, the University of Georgia, the University of Chicago, and Columbia University are the catalogues of schools which he attended as a student and at which he taught: *Annual Announcement of the University of Georgia with a Catalogue of the Officers and Students,* 1893–1900 (Atlanta, 1893–1900); University of Chicago *Annual Register*, 1897–98 (Chicago, 1898); *Catalogue of the University of Wisconsin* (title varies), 1901–1908 (Madison, 1901–1908), *Bulletin of the Tulane University of Louisiana: The Register*, 1907–11 (New Orleans, 1907–11); *Calendar of the University of Michigan* (title varies), 1910–29 (Ann Arbor, 1910–29); *Bulletin of Yale University: General Catalogue Number*, 1930–34 (New Haven, 1929–34).

Phillips has been the subject of critical appraisal in the meritorious study by Wood Gray, "Ulrich Bonnell Phillips," in William T. Hutchinson (ed.), *The Marcus W. Jernegan Essays in American Historiography* (Chicago, 1937), 354–73. For an informative typescript critique of Gray's essay the writer is indebted to Herbert A. Kellar. Fred Landon, "Ulrich Bonnell Phillips: Historian of the South," *Journal of Southern History*, V (August, 1939), 364–71, is an appreciation by a personal friend. An obituary notice appeared in the *American Historical Review*, XXXIX (July, 1934), 598–99. The essential facts of the historian's life are recorded in E. Merton Coulter, "Ulrich Bonnell Phillips," *Dictionary of American Biography*, XXI, 597–98. Philip C. Newman, "Ulrich Bonnell Phillips—The South's Foremost Historian," *Georgia Historical Quarterly* (Savannah), XXV (September, 1941), 244–61, makes a modest contribution. For an appraisal of revisionist viewpoints of slavery and for some pertinent unsolved questions concerning the institution, see Kenneth M. Stamp, "The Historian and Southern Negro Slavery," *American Historical Review*, LVII (April, 1952), 613–24. Phillips' concentration on large plantations is the theme of Richard Hofstadter, "U. B. Phillips and the Plantation Legend," *Journal of Negro History* (Washington), XXIX (April, 1944), 109–24.

Two bibliographies of Phillips' writings appeared within the year of his death: David M. Potter, Jr. (comp.),

"A Bibliography of the Printed Writings of Ulrich Bonnell Phillips," *Georgia Historical Quarterly,* XVIII (September, 1934), 270–82; Everett E. Edwards (comp.), "A Bibliography of the Writings of Professor Ulrich Bonnell Phillips," *Agricultural History* (Chicago, Baltimore), VIII (October, 1934), 196–218. An introduction to this compilation was contributed by Fred Landon. The Edwards bibliography is annotated with pertinent quotations from books and articles, with chapter titles of most of the books, and with citations to reviews in periodicals and newspapers.

Phillips wrote six volumes of southern history: *Georgia and State Rights. A Study of the Political History of Georgia from the Revolution to the Civil War, with Particular Regard to Federal Relations* (Washington, 1902); *A History of Transportation in the Eastern Cotton Belt to 1860* (New York, 1908); *The Life of Robert Toombs* (New York, 1913); *American Negro Slavery; A Survey of the Supply, Employment and Control of Negro Labor as Determined by the Plantation Régime* (New York, 1918); *Life and Labor in the Old South* (Boston, 1929); and a posthumous work, *The Course of the South to Secession; An Interpretation* (New York, 1939), edited by E. Merton Coulter. Three edited works supplemented his writings: *Plantation and Frontier,* 2 vols. (Cleveland, 1910) (the first two volumes of the cooperative ten-volume *Documentary History of American Industrial Society*); *The Correspondence of Robert Toombs, Alexander H. Stephens, and Howell Cobb,* American Historical Association *Annual Report,* 1911, II (Washington, 1913); *Florida Plantation Records from the Papers of George Noble Jones* (St. Louis, 1927), with James D. Glunt.

Many of Phillips' articles dealt with the economy of the Old South, particularly plantations and slavery. The more important contributions in this area to periodical literature were "The Economics of the Plantation," *South Atlantic Quarterly*, II (July, 1903), 231–36; "The Plantation as a Civilizing Factor," *Sewanee Review* (Sewanee, Tennessee), XII (July, 1904), 257–67; "The Economic Cost of Slaveholding in the Cotton Belt," *Political Science Quarterly*, XX (June, 1905), 257–75; "The Slave Labor Problem in the Charleston District," *Political Science Quarterly*, XXII (September, 1907), 416–39; "The Origin and Growth of Southern Black Belts," *American Historical Review*, XI (July, 1906), 798–816; "Slave Crime in Virginia," *American Historical Review*, XX (January, 1915), 336–40; "Racial Problems, Adjustments and Disturbances," *The South in the Building of the Nation*, VII, 173–99; "The Economics of Slave Labor in the South," *The South in the Building of the Nation*, V, 121–24; "The Economics of the Slave Trade, Foreign and Domestic," *The South in the Building of the Nation*, V, 124–29; "Financial Crises in the Ante-Bellum South," *The South in the Building of the Nation*, V, 435–41.

Occasionally the theme carried Phillips beyond the limits of the South: "A Jamaica Slave Plantation," *American Historical Review*, XIX (April, 1914), 543–58; "An Antigua Plantation, 1769–1818," *North Carolina Historical Review*, III (July, 1926), 439–45; "Plantations with Slave Labor and Free," *American Historical Review*, XXX (July, 1925), 738–53, an analysis of western sugar-beet ranches; "Plantations East and South of Suez," *Agricultural History*, V (July, 1931), 93–109. The last two articles surveyed present-day problems; others took a presentist view of the New South: "Conservatism and Progress in the Cotton Belt," *South Atlantic Quarterly*, III (January, 1904), 1–10; "The Overproduction of Cotton and a Possible Remedy," *South Atlantic Quarterly*, IV (April, 1905), 148–58; "Making Cotton Pay," *World's Work*, VIII (May, 1904),

4782–92; "The Decadence of the Plantation System," *Annals of the American Academy of Political and Social Science* (Philadelphia), XXXV (January, 1910), 37–41.

Conveyance absorbed Phillips' attention in "Transportation in the Ante-Bellum South: An Economic Analysis," *Quarterly Journal of Economics* (Boston, Cambridge), XIX (May, 1905), 434–51, which served as the first chapter of *A History of Transportation in the Eastern Cotton Belt to 1860*; "An American State-Owned Railroad," *Yale Review*, XV (November, 1906), 259–82, another segment of the same book; "Railroads in the South," *The South in the Building of the Nation*, V, 358–67; "Railway Transportation in the South," *The South in the Building of the Nation*, VI, 305–16.

Interest in archives dated from Phillips' years as a graduate student at the University of Georgia, and he enthusiastically accepted an assignment from the American Historical Association to survey Georgia's records. Two publications resulted: "The Public Archives of Georgia," American Historical Association *Annual Report*, 1903, I (Washington, 1904), 439–74; "Georgia's Local Archives," American Historical Association *Annual Report*, 1904 (Washington, 1905), 555–96. Personal observations rather than systematic treatment found their way into "Documentary Collections and Publication in the Older States of the South," American Historical Association *Annual Report*, 1905, I (Washington, 1906), 200–204. He edited some papers from the Draper Collection (State Historical Society of Wisconsin, Madison), to "illustrate various phases of life one hundred years ago," for publication as "Documents," *Gulf States Historical Magazine* (Montgomery), II (July, 1903), 58–60; and he contributed "Some Letters of Joseph Habersham" to the *Georgia Historical Quarterly*, X (June, 1926), 144–63.

Political history and public policy were themes that

occupied Phillips' attention in the early years of his productive career. In these areas he contributed "Georgia in
the Federal Union, 1776–1861" to *The South in the Building of the Nation,* II, 146–71; "The Slavery Issue in Federal
Politics" to *The South in the Building of the Nation,* IV,
382–422; "The South Carolina Federalists" to the *American Historical Review,* XIV (April, July, 1909), 529–43,
731–43; "The Southern Whigs, 1834–1854" to *Essays in
American History Dedicated to Frederick Jackson Turner*
(New York, 1910), 203–29; "The Literary Movement for
Secession" to *Studies in Southern History and Politics Inscribed to William Archibald Dunning* (New York, 1914),
[31]–60. Sketches of John C. Calhoun, William H. Crawford, Robert Y. Hayne, Alexander H. Stephens, and Robert
Toombs appeared in the *Dictionary of American Biography,* III, 411–19, 527–30; VIII, 456–59; XVII, 569–75;
XVIII, 590–92; brief biographies of Jefferson Davis, Stephen A. Douglas, and Toombs in the *Encyclopaedia of the
Social Sciences,* V, 11–12, 227–28; XIV, 651. To the *Encyclopaedia of the Social Sciences* he also contributed "Popular Sovereignty," XII, 239–40; and "Slavery, Modern,
United States," XIV, 84–90.

Phillips is not usually classified as an interpretive historian, and yet there was interpretation in his writings.
Sometimes it is necessary to read between the lines to discover it, for he seldom added the two and two to arrive at
the four. His philosophy of history, as well as his philosophy
of life, is readily apparent in a few of his articles and in
Life and Labor. "The Central Theme of Southern History," *American Historical Review,* XXXIV (October,
1928), 30–43, reprinted in the *Course of the South to Secession,* 151–65, identifies white supremacy as "the cardinal
test of a Southerner" and as the continuous thread that
gave unity to southern thought. The theme reappeared in
"The Historic Civilization of the South," *Agricultural*

History, XII (April, 1938), 142–50, in which Phillips became advocate as well as historian of the "white man's country" philosophy. This article, an address delivered before a joint meeting of the Institute of Rural Affairs at Virginia Polytechnic Institute and the Farmers' Institute, Blacksburg, July 28, 1931, also proclaimed Phillips' conclusion that the struggle culminating in the Civil War was a repressible conflict. A succinct statement of this interpretation was incorporated in a "Memorial Day Address" delivered at Yale University, May 30, 1931, *Yale Alumni Weekly* (New Haven), XL (June 5, 1931), 968. A Phi Beta Kappa address at Yale, "The Master Touch Is Urged on Youth," New York *Times,* March 29, 1931, sec. 3, p. 7, c. 6, gave wholesome advice to superior students. "The Traits and Contributions of Frederick Jackson Turner," an address prepared for delivery at the Toronto meeting of the American Historical Association, December 28, 1932, was published posthumously in *Agricultural History,* XIX (January, 1945), 21–23.

Two articles emanated from the historian's trip around the world in 1929–30 as Albert Kahn Fellow: "Nilotics and Azande," Albert Kahn Foundation for the Foreign Travel of American Teachers *Reports* (New York), IX (1930), 11–47; "Azandeland," *Yale Review,* N. S., XX (December, 1930), 293–313.

In the years 1903–1905 Phillips sought to influence policy in the South by advocating a reduction in cotton acreage, adjustment of the labor problem, an application of modern business methods, and a return to the plantation system. He contributed communications to sundry newspapers on these and related subjects, and they in turn published editorials and letters of approval and disapproval. Typescript copies of a considerable body of this material were provided by the *Agricultural History* office: Atlanta *Constitution,* August 24, September 1, 6, 10, 22,

24, 1903; April 3, 11, 15, 24, May 1, August 28, December 8, 16, 28, 1904; January 12, 26, 31, June 10, 27, 29, 1905; Macon *Telegraph,* September 16, 23, 27, 1904; Savannah *News,* December 30, 1904; January 5, 1905; Savannah *Press,* June 27, 1905; New York *Sun,* April 21, 1904; Vicksburg *Herald,* April 22, 1904.

Appraisals of books were significant assignments in Phillips' code. Seeking to attain precision in style and thought, he gave these shorter pieces the same painstaking attention that he accorded articles and chapters of books. Phillips reviewed an average of three books every two years; these he contributed to the *American Historical Review,* the *Mississippi Valley Historical Review,* the Southern History Association *Publications,* the *North Carolina Historical Review,* the *Sewanee Review,* the *Annals of the American Academy of Political and Social Science,* the *Gulf States Historical Magazine,* and the *Yale Review.*

Walter Lynwood Fleming

The Walter Lynwood Fleming Collection in the New York Public Library is the largest assemblage of the historian's papers. These consist of transcripts of the Black Codes of France and Louisiana; manuscripts of his writings, accompanied by reprints, and notes and correspondence connected with their composition; transcripts of General William Tecumseh Sherman's correspondence, 1859–91; material on the Ku Klux Klan, the Negro, and Negro schools; correspondence and other papers assembled for a biography of Jefferson Davis; typewritten copies of syllabuses on the history of slavery and Reconstruction of seceded states; and the diary of William L. Brown of Montgomery County, Tennessee, 1805–14. Extant notes on subjects Fleming investigated are not numerous. Lack of system prevailed: most of them are on half sheets, a few of which are typed; others are on three-by-five slips, still others on four-by-six cards. The collection also contains scores of illustrations assembled for the uncompleted biography of Davis.

Among the letters in the New York Public Library Collection are communications to or from Myrta Lockett Avery, Guy C. Callender, John W. DuBose, A. V. Goodpasture, Armistead C. Gordon, Amelia G. Gorgas, Hinton R. Helper, Hilary A. Herbert, Walter H. Page, Albert C. Phelps, Milo M. Quaife, John C. Reed, Dunbar Rowland, Yates Snowden, Alfred H. Stone, John Wilson Townsend, Benjamin C. Truman, and Oswald Garrison Villard.

Three small collections of Fleming Papers are available. The Official Files, Chancellor's Office, Vanderbilt University, Nashville, includes considerable Fleming material, 1917–31, relating mainly to his period as dean of the College of Arts and Sciences and especially to the Social Science Division and its development through the Laura Spelman Rockefeller Memorial. Through the courtesy of Dr. William C. Binkley, use was made of a file of letters, reports, and records, 1925–29 (housed in his office at Vanderbilt University, 1944), relating mainly to Fleming's work as dean of the college. This collection also contains Pocket Notebooks Nos. 1–4, the first and second probably for the West Virginia University period, the third and fourth for the Louisiana State University years. In these he recorded such miscellanea as outlines of lectures, thesis topics, reading lists, names and addresses of persons who might provide information on subjects he was investigating, and lists of Klan members. Transcripts of four Fleming letters, 1903–1904, written to Dr. G. P. L. Reed, a Marion, Alabama, physician, were provided through the courtesy of Dr. Weymouth T. Jordan. The originals are on file in the Historic Room, Judson College, Marion.

Other manuscript collections contain Fleming correspondence: the Adams, Boyd, Dodd, Hamilton, Snowden, and American Historical Association Papers; Departmental Correspondence and Papers in the Maps and Manuscripts Room, Alabama Department of Archives and History; Dunbar Rowland Papers in the Mississippi Department of Archives and History, Jackson; William Garrott Brown Papers, Manuscript Division, Duke University Library; George P. Garrison Papers, Archives Collection, University of Texas Library.

The transcript of Fleming's record from the registrar's office, Columbia University, is a technical aid in visualizing breadth of graduate training. For George Petrie's philosophy of history and for course offerings at Auburn, see *Catalogue of the State Agricultural and Mechanical College, Alabama Polytechnic Institute* (title varies), 1887–1901 (Auburn, Montgomery, [1887]–1901); for course offerings at Columbia and at schools upon whose faculties Fleming served, see *Columbia University Catalogue,* 1900–1904 (New York, 1899–1904); *West Virginia University Bulletin,* 1903–1907 (Morgantown, 1903–1907); *Louisiana State University Catalogue,* 1907–17 (Baton Rouge, New Orleans, 1907–1917); *Register of Vanderbilt University,* 1917–28 (Nashville, 1917–1928).

Of Fleming's book-length publications, four involved the writing rather than the compilation of history: *Civil War and Reconstruction in Alabama* (New York, 1905); *The Sequel of Appomattox; A Chronicle of the Reunion of the States* (New Haven, 1919); *The Freedmen's Savings Bank; A Chapter in the Economic History of the Negro Race* (Chapel Hill, 1927); *Louisiana State University, 1860–1896* (Baton Rouge, 1936). His first edited work of book length consisted of eight numbers of *Documents Relating to Reconstruction* (Morgantown, 1904); followed soon by a new edition of John C. Lester and D. L. Wilson, *Ku Klux Klan. Its Origin, Growth and Disbandment* (New York,

1905), valuable for the introduction and the appendixes as well as the reproduction of the text. His greatest contribution as an editor, however, was the *Documentary History of Reconstruction, Political, Military, Social, Religious, Educational & Industrial, 1865 to the Present Time*, 2 vols. (Cleveland, 1906–1907). Another work had considerable value: *General W. T. Sherman as College President. A collection of letters, documents, and other material, chiefly from private sources, relating to the life and activities of General William Tecumseh Sherman, to the early years of Louisiana State University, and to the stirring conditions existing in the South on the eve of the Civil War: 1859–1861* (Cleveland, 1912). A syllabus, *The Reconstruction of the Seceded States, 1865–1876* (Albany, 1905) consisted of an outline, illustrative materials, and a bibliography.

Anyone wishing a complete list of Fleming's articles, bulletins, and reprints will do well to consult Fletcher M. Green, "Walter Lynwood Fleming: Historian of Reconstruction," *Journal of Southern History*, II (November, 1936), 497–521, valuable especially for its annotated bibliography. Fleming's contributions on the life of Jefferson Davis are valuable segments of an uncompleted task: "Jefferson Davis at West Point," Mississippi Historical Society *Publications* (University, Oxford, Jackson), X (1909), 247–67; "Jefferson Davis' First Marriage," Mississippi Historical Society *Publications*, XII (1912), 21–36; "Jefferson Davis, the Negroes and the Negro Problem," *Sewanee Review*, XVI (October, 1908), 407–27; "Jefferson Davis's Camel Experiment," *Popular Science Monthly* (New York), LXXIV (February, 1909), 141–52; "The Religious Life of Jefferson Davis," *Methodist Quarterly Review* (Louisville, Nashville), LIX (April, 1910), 325–42; "The Early Life of Jefferson Davis," Mississippi Valley Historical Association *Proceedings*, 1915–18 (Cedar Rapids), IX (1919), 151–76; "Concerning Jefferson Davis," *Bookman*, LIX (March,

1924), 82–85; and two documentary collections: "Two Important Letters by Jefferson Davis Discovered," Southern Historical Society *Papers* (Richmond), XXXIV (1908), 8–12; "Some Documents Relating to Jefferson Davis at West Point," *Mississippi Valley Historical Review,* VII (September, 1921), 146–52. Several of these studies were reprinted as *Bulletins of Louisiana State University* (Baton Rouge).

Fleming's research on his dissertation resulted in the publication of several articles relating to his native state: "The Peace Movement in Alabama During the Civil War: Party Politics, 1861–1864," *South Atlantic Quarterly,* II (April, 1903), 114–24; "The Peace Movement in Alabama During the Civil War: The Peace Society, 1863–1865," *South Atlantic Quarterly,* II (July, 1903), 246–60; "Industrial Development in Alabama During the Civil War," *South Atlantic Quarterly,* III (July, 1904), 260–72; "Blockade Running and Trade Through the Lines into Alabama, 1861–1865," *South Atlantic Quarterly,* IV (July, 1905), 256–72; "The Churches of Alabama During the Civil War and Reconstruction," *Gulf States Historical Magazine,* I (September, 1902), 105–27; "The Formation of the Union League in Alabama," *Gulf States Historical Magazine,* II (September, 1903), 73–89; "The Ku Klux Testimony Relating to Alabama," *Gulf States Historical Magazine,* II (November, 1903), 155–60; "Conscription and Exemption in Alabama During the Civil War," *Gulf States Historical Magazine,* II (March-May, 1904), 310–25; "Home Life in Alabama During the Civil War," Southern History Association *Publications,* VIII (1904), 81–103; "Reconstruction in Alabama," *The South in the Building of the Nation,* II, 292–311; "Reorganization of the Industrial System in Alabama After the Civil War," *American Journal of Sociology,* X (January, 1905), 473–99; "Military Government in Alabama, 1865–1866," *American Historical Magazine and Ten-*

nessee Historical Society Quarterly (Nashville), VIII (April, 1903), 163–79; "Military Government in Alabama Under the Reconstruction Acts," *American Historical Magazine and Tennessee Historical Society Quarterly,* VIII (July, 1903), 222–52, "The Servant Problem in a Black Belt Village," *Sewanee Review,* XIII (January, 1905), 1–17.

Other articles, some of them with an Alabama background, were built on a broader framework or concerned other states: "The Buford Expedition to Kansas," *American Historical Review,* VI (October, 1900), 38–48, republished in expanded form in the Alabama Historical Society *Transactions* (Montgomery), IV (1904), 167–92; "Louisiana During the War Between the States and the Reconstruction, 1861–1867," *The South in the Building of the Nation,* III, 134–62; "The Reconstruction, 1862–1877," *The South in the Building of the Nation,* IV, 579–626; "The Slave-Labor System in the Ante-Bellum South," *The South in the Building of the Nation,* V, 104–20; "The Labor Force and Labor Conditions, 1861–1865," *The South in the Building of the Nation,* V, 146–51; "The Economic Conditions During the Reconstruction," *The South in the Building of the Nation,* VI, 1–11; "The Economic Results of the Reconstruction," *The South in the Building of the Nation,* VI, 12–16; "Labor and Labor Conditions," *The South in the Building of the Nation,* VI, 41–48; "The Effect of the Reconstruction on Property Values in the South," *The South in the Building of the Nation,* VI, 390–93; "Changes in Property Values Since Reconstruction," *The South in the Building of the Nation,* VI, 393–96; "The Independent Order of White Men," *South Atlantic Quarterly,* IV (January, 1905), 78–81; "Ex-Slave Pension Frauds," *South Atlantic Quarterly,* IX (April, 1910), 123–35; "William Tecumseh Sherman as College President," *South Atlantic Quarterly,* XI (January, 1912), 33–54; "Forty Acres and a Mule," *North American*

Review (Boston, New York), CLXXXII (May, 1906), 721–37; "The Freedmen's Savings Bank," *Yale Review,* XV (May, August, 1906), 40–67, 134–46; "Immigration to the Southern States," *Political Science Quarterly,* XX (June, 1905), 276–97; "Italian Farm Labor in the South," *World Today* (Chicago), VII (September, 1904), 1232–33; "Immigration and the Negro Problem," *World Today,* XII (January, 1907), 96–97; "The Religious and Hospitable Rite of Feet Washing," *Sewanee Review,* XVI (January, 1908), 1–13; "Deportation and Colonization: An Attempted Solution of the Race Problem," *Studies in Southern History and Politics Inscribed to William Archibald Dunning,* [1]–30; "The Memoirs of James Murray Mason, Confederate Commissioner to England," Southern History Association *Publications,* VIII (1904), 465–72; " 'Pap' Singleton, The Moses of the Colored Exodus," *American Journal of Sociology,* XV (July, 1909), 61–82; "The Public Career of Robert Livingston," *New York Genealogical and Biographical Record* (New York), XXXII (July, October, 1901), 129–35, 194–200.

The fifty-nine brief articles which Fleming contributed to dictionaries and encyclopedias are too numerous for separate listing. They are, for the most part, biographical sketches of Southerners and factual accounts of southern events, movements, and institutions. Over half of them appeared in the biographical volumes of *The South in the Building of the Nation,* XI–XII; the others in the *Dictionary of American Biography;* the *Cyclopedia of American Government;* the *Encyclopedia Americana,* 30 vols. (New York, 1924); the *Encyclopaedia Britannica,* 29 vols. (11th ed., Cambridge, 1911); the *Encyclopaedia Britannica,* 24 vols. (14th ed., London, 1929); and *Nelson's Perpetual Loose Leaf Encyclopaedia,* 12 vols. (New York, 1905–30). Fleming contributed book reviews to the *American Histori-*

cal Review, the *Mississippi Valley Historical Review,* the *Political Science Quarterly,* and the Southern History Association *Publications.*

A factual sketch of Fleming's career is available in Fletcher M. Green, "Walter Lynwood Fleming," *Dictionary of American Biography,* XXI, 302–303. The bibliography in Green, "Walter Lynwood Fleming: Historian of Reconstruction," *Journal of Southern History,* II (November, 1936), 497–521, is preceded by an appraisal of the historian's work. William C. Binkley, "The Contribution of Walter Lynwood Fleming to Southern Scholarship," *Journal of Southern History,* V (May, 1939), 143–54, is a penetrating analysis of conceptual development and of waning productivity after 1912. Valuable notes are available in Miss Robbie Smith Sparks, "A Handbook of the Alabama Polytechnic Institute" (M.S. thesis, Alabama Polytechnic Institute, 1935); in Marcus M. Wilkerson, *Thomas Duckett Boyd; The Story of a Southern Educator* (Baton Rouge, 1935); and in two books by Edwin Mims, *Chancellor Kirkland of Vanderbilt* (Nashville, 1940), and *History of Vanderbilt University* (Nashville, 1946). The writer has drawn upon "Some Pioneer Alabama Historians": "Walter L. Fleming," *Alabama Review,* I (October, 1948), 261–78, for considerable data; to a lesser extent upon "George Petrie," *Alabama Review,* I (July, 1948), 164–79; and "Thomas M. Owen," *Alabama Review,* II (January, 1949), 45–62.

Index

Abbott, Lyman, *Outlook* editor, 49–50; Dodd characterizes, 50

Absconding, among slaves, 82–84

Adams, Charles Francis, 43; liberal attitude of toward southern view of Reconstruction, 19–20; reviews Dodd's *Jefferson Davis*, 41

Adams, Henry, 13, 15; counsels Alderman, 14; treats southern Federalists inadequately, 79

Adams, Herbert Baxter, 2, 5, 6, 22, 33, 98–99; attracts southern students to Hopkins, 1; influences Petrie, 96; seminar of, 21, 25, 80

Adams, John, 47

Africanization, imperils white supremacy, 92

Agriculture, southern, stressed by Phillips, 75

Alabama, buys few books on Alabama, 103

Alabama Historical Society, 10

Alabama Historical Society *Transactions*, Fleming contributes to, 98

Alabama Polytechnic Institute, 2; advanced educational methods of, 97; Fleming attends, 96–98

Alabama State Department of Archives and History, 10; founded by Owen, 25; liberal policy of, 102

Alderman, Edwin A., 15; seeks distinguishing southern characteristics, 12–15

American Bureau of Industrial Research, inaugurated by Ely, 73

American Commonwealth, by James Bryce, 49

American Epoch, by Howard W. Odum, criticized by Phillips, 76

American Historical Association, 7,

117; Dodd attends annual meetings of, 35; invited to South, 9, 11–12; New Orleans meeting of, 11; sponsors southern history sessions, 8, 11

American Historical Magazine and Tennessee Historical Society Quarterly, 16

American Historical Review, 11, 16, 41; appraises southern books, 18; Dodd contributes to, 35; edited by Jameson, 65; Fleming contributes to, 98, 103; Phillips contributes to, 71

American leadership, qualifications for, 47

American Negro Slave Revolts, by Herbert Aptheker, criticizes Phillips, 85

American Negro Slavery, by Ulrich B. Phillips, 74, 78; cites Olmsted, 78; used as text, 25–26

American sectionalism, Turner's lecture on influences Phillips, 64

Americanism, virtue of southern and western, 48

Andrew Jackson, by James Parton, 17

Andrew Jackson, by William Garrott Brown, 17

Andrews, Charles M., 2; appraises *South Atlantic Quarterly*, 18–19

Anti-Slavery Crusade, by Jesse Macy, used as text, 26

Appomattox, 91

Aptheker, Herbert, *American Negro Slave Revolts*, 85

Aristocracy, leisure among, 89; northern urban, 44; Phillips his-

INDEX

151

Chapel Hill, hosts American Historical Association, 12

Charleston, hosts American Historical Association, 11

Charleston-Beaufort region, controlled by plantation lords, 42

Chattanooga, hosts American Historical Association, 12

Chicago, University of, 21; Dodd accepts position at, 35; Phillips attends summer session at, 63–64, 75

Chronicles of America, 40, 105

Churchill, Winston (N. H.), 13

Circuit rider, in Georgia, 62

Civil War, 80, 110; carnage, 90–91; causes, 12–13, 90–91; consequences, 80, 91–92; Fleming corresponds with contemporaries of, 112; history of at Columbia, 64

Civil War and Reconstruction in Alabama, by Walter L. Fleming, 95, 104, 105, 111; comprehensive nature of, 115; criticized by Du Bois, 118; personalized character of, 115; shortcomings of, 115

Civilization, southern, attributes of, 92

Clay, Henry, 35, 45

Clayton, N. C., Dodd attends high school at, 29; Dodd teaches private school at, 30

Cleveland, Grover, allied with moneyed interests, 44

Columbia University, 2, 21, 22, 58, 64, 80, 111; Fleming attends, 99; Phillips attends, 64–65; southern history center, 5, 6, 99

Columbia University Press Committee on Publication, objects to dedication in Phillips' *Transportation in the Eastern Cotton Belt,* 72

Columbia University *Studies in History, Economics and Public Law,* 15

Common man, Dodd's faith in, 45

Concubinage, 84

Confederacy, history of, 6–7; veterans protest Dodd's preachments on, 41

Confederate Collection, University of Texas, 25

Confederate Museum, New Orleans, denies free use of collection, 101

Connor, Henry G., 19–20

Conservatism, southern, 3, 4, 18, 95, 99, 105, 115, 116, 118, 119

Correspondence of Robert Toombs, Alexander H. Stephens, and Howell Cobb, edited by Ulrich B. Phillips, 70

Cosmos Club, 51

Cotterill, Robert S., *Old South,* 26

Cotton culture, 60

Cotton Kingdom, by William E. Dodd, appraised, 40; used as text, 26

Cotton Kingdom, Phillips' interest in, 83

"Could and ought the Southern Confederacy have Succeeded?" by L. M. Pipkin, 110

Course of the South to Secession, by Ulrich B. Phillips, 70

Court records, as historical sources, 78, 89–90

Cox, James M., corresponds with Dodd, 51–52

Craven, Avery, appraises Dodd's teaching, 37–38

Crawford, William H., Phillips gathers material for biography of, 71

"Creed of the Old South," by Basil L. Gildersleeve, 12–13

Critical Study of Nullification in South Carolina, by David F. Houston, 14, 16

Daniels, Josephus, corresponds with Dodd, 52; recommends Dodd for West Point, 29–30

Davis, Jefferson, 32, 35, 39, 43, 45, 71, 106, 107, 108, 109, 110, 111; criticism of, 109–10; Fleming's research on, 101, 106–11; *Rise and Fall of the Confederate Government,* 110

Davis, John W., Democratic presidential candidate, 52

Davis, William Watson, member of Dunning "school," 6